Nothing Silent Anymore

Healing in the Open: Learning to Understand & Overcome Childhood and Adult Trauma

By: Ebony Mitchem

Nothing Silent Anymore

Contents

Take Another Look in The Mirror 4

    Introduction Forged by Fire, Guided by Grace 6

    Chapter 1 Anxiety and Depression Weighing In 8

    Chapter 2 The Weight of Silence 17

    Chapter 3 My First Eviction Experience 24

    Chapter 4 A Hard Knock Life 34

    Chapter 5 Trading Fear for Hustle: My Sister's Legacy 49

    Chapter 6 Silent No More 57

    Chapter 7 Unraveled Bonds 77

    Chapter 8 When CPS Entered Our Lives 87

    Chapter 9 Kicking Me While I am Down 97

    Chapter 10 Rage Igniting: A Mother's Resolve 105

    Chapter 11 Suicide Cannot Have My Life 116

    Chapter 12 Change My Life 127

Chapter 13 Breaking Free from Shame and Fear 137

    Chapter 14 Game Changer 161

    Acknowledgements 171

Take Another Look in The Mirror

Growing up you look in the mirror and be disgusted with yourself...
Meaning you had a profound disapproval of yourself.

You would sit there and shame yourself because your heart was filled with pain that was caused by another human beings not only wrong but foolish behaviors.

You then take another look and blame yourself, because you had then assigned to yourself the responsibility of one's wrongful actions.

Man, that pain you felt made you not only seek but cry.
Cry and seek help silently from just one solid person who would listen to your truth.

They still do not understand that due to your fear of humiliation, you held a fear of being put in a lower position in the eyes of others. So, you could not even trust anyone to have the conversation.

You thought that isolation would help but that then turned into a suicide attempt, where you had then caused harm to yourself hoping that was the end to the pain in your life.

That suicide attempt is what gave you strength, to gain the power to be physically, mentally, and emotionally strong enough to fight a battle that was only yours.

Today when you look in that mirror, I want you to congratulate yourself, give praise to yourself daily, and add positive affirmations filled with words of encouragement to keep your spirit uplifted.

Why? Because you no longer have a reason to blame, be disgusted, and ashamed of yourself.

Now I want you to take another look in the mirror and it will show you the need to protect, love, and care for yourself more than you ever have. Because you are more than enough.

Introduction

Forged by Fire, Guided by Grace

Every story has a beginning. Mine started in north-central Kentucky. I grew up living on my dreams, hopes, and the hard lessons of not allowing circumstances beyond my control to dictate my path. As a child, I often felt ashamed of situations I couldn't change—poverty felt like an unjust judgment, something I couldn't prove or dispel, despite my family's constant struggles. The systems meant to uplift often seemed designed to hold us down, repeatedly pulling us under just as we fought to break through.

The cycle of eviction and instability became a grim familiarity in my youth, embedding itself in my memories like a recurring nightmare. Yet, despite the bitterness that simmered within me for years, I've come to understand that my mother navigated these challenges with incredible resilience and determination. She did the best she could with what little she had, and her strength in the face of adversity became a guiding light for me.

Through the hardships of my childhood and into adulthood, I never allowed those circumstances to define me or keep me down when life became rough. When faced with setbacks like losing my job after a fraud investigation or experiencing a severe mental breakdown, I made a conscious decision to seek therapy and reclaim my life. "I will kill them with success," became my mantra—a determination to rise above the challenges that threatened to overwhelm me.

Therapy became crucible where I confronted past traumas and current struggles head-on. It was a process of unraveling the layers of physical, mental, sexual, and emotional abuse that had shaped my insecurities. In that journey, I learned the power of education, professional guidance, persistence, and self-discipline in reshaping my life. These tools became my pathway to healing and personal growth, enabling me to forge a new path forward.

As a mother now, I carry these lessons with me, determined to break the cycle of silence and stigma. I openly discuss my past with my children, explaining the challenges we faced and the resilience that carried us through. Nothing remains hidden or unspoken because I believe in the power of honesty and understanding to build resilience in the face of adversity. My children will know that despite the hardships, we can rise, learn, and grow stronger together.

Chapter 1
Anxiety and Depression Weighing In

In the journey of life, nothing holds greater importance than your mental well-being. I learned this truth the hard way, realizing that relying on others who could not comprehend my struggles only perpetuated the feeling that my truth was a lie. It is common to face mental health challenges, and I refuse to hide mine. Anxiety, depression, and PTSD have been part of my story since my earliest memories. Yet, it was not until I stepped into therapy that I began confronting the shadows of my past. Admitting my vulnerabilities was not easy; I feared judgment and rejection. But it was in the quiet space of therapy, where honesty and transparency were demanded, that I found the courage to peel back the layers of my trauma. I will never forget the moment my therapist asked about my childhood, my mother, my father, and things that caused trauma. It was a conversation I had avoided for years, a wound I had kept buried deep within. Who would have imagined that the source of my pain came from a person who was meant to love and protect me?

My story strongly corresponds with the social work competency of "Engagement" in the larger context of the Core Competencies of the NASW (National Association of Social Workers). Engaging clients means developing a relationship, earning their trust, and encouraging candid conversation. In my narrative, my involvement in therapy is characterized as a journey towards mental health rehabilitation. I go through my early anxieties of being judged and rejected and find the confidence to be vulnerable and face my trauma in the therapeutic session. This is a perfect example of how a social workers can provide a secure and encouraging space where I felt free to discuss my feelings and experiences. The proof is in how therapy changed my life; through meaningful interaction with my therapist, I was able to gain understanding and start to mend from old traumas.

Therapy Session

Therapist: Good morning. Ebony, I want to encourage you to explore the depths of your past, to speak your truth about your childhood, your parents, and the experiences that have caused you pain.

Me: It's hard to even know where to begin. There are so many layers to unravel.

Therapist: I understand. It's okay to take it one step at a time. Let's start with whatever feels most pressing for you.

Me: Well, I guess... I guess I need to talk about my mother. She was supposed to be my rock, my protector. But instead, I felt she turned a blind eye to the things that has happened to me.

Therapist: That sounds incredibly painful. It's okay to feel angry or betrayed by her actions, or lack thereof.

Me: And my father—you know, he was never really there? I also harbor some negative memory of him. Where a father's love and guidance should have been, there seems to be an imbalance.

Therapist: It's common for neglect or emotional absence from a parent to leave a lasting impact. You deserved so much more than what you received.

Me: Yeah... I just... I never imagined that the source of all this pain would come from the people who were supposed to love and protect me.

Therapist: It's a painful realization, but acknowledging it is the first step towards healing. Being honest and transparent about your experiences allows us to work through them together, to find healing and restoration.

Me: Thank you... I never realized how much weight I was carrying until I started opening up about it. It's like... like a weight has been lifted.

Therapist: You're welcome. Remember, you are not alone in this journey. We're here to support you every step of the way. Keep going I'm just going to take a few notes.

I've told myself over and over I was just a helpless toddler, and I found myself caught in a nightmare of confusion and agony that would haunt me for a lifetime. It all began with a simple accident — a natural and innocent act that any child might engage in. However, the response from my caregiver was anything but innocent. Instead of understanding and compassion, I was met with screams and yells, as if I had committed some unforgivable offense. I could not comprehend what I had done wrong; I was just a child, after all. But the punishment that followed was beyond my comprehension. I was forcibly submerged in a bathtub filled with icy water until my small body turned blue, a cruel tactic meant to drive home some elusive lesson. And then, as if the torment had not been enough, I was exposed to the searing heat of a Kersen heater, scalding my tender skin, and leaving behind the physical and emotional scars that would shape my existence.

This harrowing ordeal, inflicted upon me by those meant to nurture and protect, shattered the very foundation of trust and safety that every child deserves. It was not just the physical pain of second, third, and fourth degree burns that lingered; it was the deep-seated insecurity and fear that gnawed at my soul, even as I grew into adulthood. Despite their intentions, my caregivers misguided actions served only to exacerbate the trauma, leaving me adrift in a sea of profound pain and psychological distress. For years, I struggled to make sense of the senseless, unable to fully heal from the wounds inflicted upon me during my most vulnerable years. And so, the scars of that fateful day remain etched upon my psyche, a constant reminder of the unfathomable cruelty that can lurk behind the facade of love and care.

Imagine having to learn how to walk all over again because of a single, harrowing moment that haunts your every step. For me, that moment was being subjected to extreme punishment as a toddler, left with those second, third, and fourth degree burns after a misguided disciplinary action. The scalding pain and trauma not only forced me to endure physical rehabilitation but also rewired my emotional landscape, leaving me isolated and withdrawn. That memory played on repeat in my mind like a relentless video loop, each step a painful reminder of the agony and fear I experienced. It is a journey of resilience and survival, navigating through the wreckage of my past to reclaim my sense of self and find solace in the healing process.

Picture the weight of a memory so haunting, it is like a relentless anchor, dragging you down into a sea of pain and fear each time it resurfaces. This is the reality I confront—a reality where I must summon every ounce of bravery to unveil my story, not to incite guilt or shame, but to cast a beacon on the profound scars of trauma. Can you grasp the anguish of being deceived, your truth twisted and obscured, while the vivid recollections persist like unwelcome guests? Resilience is created in the furnace of my past's darkest corners during this journey, where finding comfort in vulnerability turns into a defiant act against the darkness. In the realm of social work, it's a testament to the power of empathy and understanding in healing the wounds of the past and empowering others to reclaim their narratives.

I confronted my accuser twice, which calls for a bravery that goes beyond simple bravery; it called for a resolute commitment to facing the ghosts of the past and regaining my own agency and dignity. During these crucial times, I felt like I was on the edge of panic and anxiety, carrying the burden of unsolved trauma and unanswered questions. But in the middle of all of this chaos, I found an unanticipated source of strength: the power of discussion. Even though it was challenging, talking with my accuser gave me a chance to speak up again, tell the truth, and find comfort in the search for understanding and closure. I chose to accept the only half-truths that I was given consciously, not because I was naive or hopeless, but rather because it was evidence of my unshakeable will to let go of my resentment and accept forgiveness.

I sought direction and comfort from a higher power when I was at my most miserable. I prayed to God for the ability to forgive and the calmness to find peace in the middle of the storm, my heart heavy with hurt and my spirit exhausted from the weight of the past. I discovered a renewed sense of fortitude and understanding as a result of this submission to divine grace; I realized that real healing is found in the ability to overcome suffering rather than in its absence. I was freed from the bonds of bitterness and resentment and regained my agency by letting go of the weight of resentment and accepting the transformative power of forgiveness. In this sacred act of surrender, I realized the profound truth that true power is found not in vengeance or revenge, but in the brave decision to extend grace and compassion to oneself and others.

I learned the painful lesson of silence as a child so, I had to swallow my reality, bury my feelings, and hide my suffering. This poisonous quiet turned into a blanket that smothered my voice and prevented me from being truly authentic in my expression. However, as I moved through life, I became aware of the severe toll this silence took on my wellbeing. I felt alone, devalued, and cut off from my own humanity as a result. Now that I am navigating the difficulties of recovery and self-discovery, I see how critical it is to end these generational curses. I should not sentence my children to repeat the traumas of my past or leave them with the responsibilities of my silence. We enable ourselves and future generations to create pathways of healing, authenticity, and resilience by tearing down the walls of silence and embracing vulnerability. I decided to be the change agent, writing a new chapter in my children's lives that will allow them to flourish free from the baggage of my history.

Chapter 2
The Weight of Silence

Even though I grew up in my grandmother's 37th Street house, I was burdened by childhood trauma. Fear became a constant companion for me since I was frequently left alone with other youngsters, one of whom was an intimidating teenager. There were threats, informing me that raising my voice would only cause hurt and incredulity. I fought through years of bewilderment and shame when I finally found the strength to speak out about my suffering. How could I come to terms with being taken advantage of by someone who was supposed to take care of and shield me?

I was sexually assaulted as a child by a family member, and the trauma left me with deep wounds that have affected every aspect of my life. There were serious emotional and psychological effects in addition to the physical abuse. My trust was damaged in the exact setting where it was supposed to grow, making it difficult for me to build strong bonds with people and ask for help.

Misplaced shame and guilt caused me much distress, warping my perception of myself and my value.

I isolated myself socially out of fear of being judged or disbelieved if I talk about my experience. Knowing I was forced to perform tasks that no child should have to perform, a traumatic event that left me with deep emotional wounds. In the field of social work, I have discovered how crucial it is to identify and attend to a child's long-term emotional and psychological needs in addition to their urgent safety concerns. Creating a secure environment for a child to express themselves, receive affirmation, and receive support that can be crucial in assisting them in navigating the difficult path to self-healing and restoration.

The burden of those events increased throughout the years, bearing down on me like an inflexible shadow. My mind turned into a battleground where flimsy dreams and horrors clashed. Deeper than any physical damage, my emotional injuries left me adrift in a sea of hopelessness. I carried the physical scars from those horrific wrongdoings and my body was a canvas covered in the colors of pain. Pains and aches spoke in hushed tones of suffering, silent witnesses to the evils done to me. However, it was the invisible injuries that caused the most profound damage, the breaks in security and trust that destroyed my sense of self.

I became into a ghost in the world of society, lingering in the halls of everyday life. I pulled back into the safety of silence, unable to cross the gap between my reality and what the outside world saw. I felt imprisoned in my own loneliness as every charge of lying did nothing but strengthen the barriers surrounding my heart.

Having to speak about having my own relative forcefully make me perform oral sex on him got difficult. I heard others talk about these topics with what seemed like ease, but I personally got lost in the maze of uncertainty and denial. How could I speak when my words were turned into weapons against me?

However, writing this just served to highlight the bravery, fortitude, and self-assurance required for someone to speak up and not feel embarrassed or hesitant to share your story.

When a person has experienced the trauma of sexual assault, dread can change from being just an emotion to an unwanted but enduring companion. It seeps into relationships, behaviors, and thoughts, becoming a part of life itself. Fear is a persistent emotion that creates anticipation of impending dangers and whispers memories of past horrors. It can take on a variety of shapes, including fears of closeness, vulnerability, trust, and rejection or judgment. This dread has the power to stifle, controlling decisions and influencing views. However, it can also act as a warning indicator, a well-honed survival sense during the healing process. Fear became my teacher instead of a dictator, leading me the survivor back to empowerment and the restoration of my sense of safety and autonomy via self-compassion, treatment, and support.

Silence again weighed down on my mental health like an unseen anchor, smothering the soul and lowering the brightness of hope. My mind turned into a battlefield in the dark, where worries ran wild and memories fester. One thing I do know that in the midst of the darkness, therapy shined like a light of healing, providing a safe haven where the soul can unravel its tangled web of suffering. The weight of silence has lifted, and its heavy chains broken one by one with the gentle help of my caring therapist.

My therapist replied, "You're doing an incredible job opening up," in a steady, upbeat tone. "You have a powerful way of describing your experiences, and people could really identify with it. Have you ever considered penning this tale? It might encourage and uplift people who have had comparable difficulties.

Even though I was still feeling vulnerable, I hesitated, but her words gave me the feeling of bravery.

"Keep speaking," she said, bending forward a little. "I'm here to listen, and together, we can untangle the rest of what feels overwhelming."

Her words of support were like a lifeline in the dark, urging me to press on. So, I began to expose the weight and explain how it affected me.

Exposing the Weight: Comprehending the Significance of Quiet

- ❖ Impact on Mental Health: The weight of silence had a significant negative impact on my mental health, increasing feelings of loneliness, anxiety, and sadness. My psychological anguish worsens because the feelings and painful events were suppressed and there was nowhere to express them.

- ❖ Communication Barriers: Both inwardly and externally, silence erects the obstacles to successful communication. I found it difficult to express my ideas and feelings on an internal level, which left me to feel unheard or misinterpreted. On the outside, I was afraid of others' opinions or unbelief, which kept me from talking about my experiences and made me feel even more alone.

- ❖ Physical Manifestations: The weight of silence took on physical manifestations in addition to emotional ones. Headaches, gastrointestinal disorders, and sleep disruptions are just a few of the physical health problems that attributed to my unresolved trauma and chronic stress.

- ❖ Relationship Stress: Being silent cause problems in my relationships as it leads to a lack of communication or an inability to build connections and trust. When one person in a relationship is unable or reluctant to express what they're feeling and thinking, it can lead to misunderstandings, resentment, and a breakdown in intimacy.

- ❖ Healing using Expression: One of the most important first steps on the road to rehabilitation and healing for me was to speak up. I started processing my feelings, get perspectives, and regain a sense of agency and empowerment by admitting and sharing my experiences. Finding ways to express myself whether though counseling, art, or support groups, was incredibly healing in helping me to let go of the weight of silence and regain my voice.

Chapter 3
My First Eviction Experience

When I first heard the word that would change every part of my life, eviction, I was around eleven years old and on the cusp between childhood and adolescence. I had no idea what that meant at the moment. The term had a strange, heavy, frightening sound, like a storm cloud building just over the horizon. No one gave me an explanation, but I heard it murmured in adult voices, with stress in their tones. The unexpected appearance of cardboard boxes, the quick packing of possessions, and the tears that streaked my mother's face when she believed no one was looking instead left me to figure out its meaning.

Eviction wasn't something that just happened to us; it came like a thief in the night and stole the stability I had taken for granted from our house. One day I was playing in the backyard, and the next I was looking at our belongings scattered across the front lawn, like the contents of a jar that had been knocked over. It seemed unreal, like if I had entered someone else's nightmare.

However, this was my reality. I could sense the change—the earth beneath me was no longer solid, and the concept of home would never feel the same again—even though I was not yet aware of the significance of that moment or how profoundly it would mold me.

As a sixth grader, the innocence of childhood shielded my understanding of the harsher truths of the world. When eviction disrupted my life for the first time, it shattered the fragile sense of security I had known within our home. I recall the confusion that filled my young mind as stacks of moving boxes and whispered arguments became the unsettling backdrop of my day. The word "eviction" forced me to confront a reality where stability was fleeting, and home was no longer a sanctuary.

The vibrant rhythms of school and play were abruptly overshadowed by uncertainty, leaving me wondering where we would go and whether we would ever feel safe again. Our once-harmonious household grew tense as relatives arrived in the midst of the chaos, amplifying the discord. I often retreated to quiet corners, where I could hear my older siblings' hushed arguments through the walls. Their strained voices, filled with worry and frustration, contrasted sharply with the joyful laughter that had once echoed through our home where we once shared Sunday dinners and family game nights.

The constant arguments fractured our family's bond, leaving me feeling small and powerless to mend the growing divides. As one of the youngest, I absorbed the weight of everyone's concerns. My mother's voice, edged with desperation as she tried to chart a way forward, echoed in my ears. The comfort I once took for granted dissolved, replaced by a gnawing sense of unease that marked my early years with instability and loss.

I vividly remember the morning the sheriff arrived at precisely nine, just as my mother had warned. Peeking through the curtains, I saw the landlord standing outside, his wife by his side, their stern expressions casting a shadow over our already fragile sense of security. When they began removing our belongings and unceremoniously tossing them into the yard, it felt like a brutal display of power over our vulnerability.

My mother's eyes, filled with grief and defiance, betrayed the pain of losing everything she had worked so hard to build. As the landlord's harsh words cut through the air, I felt a surge of anger and helplessness. I wanted to shield her from the humiliation and injustice of that moment, but I was just a child, unable to fight against the overwhelming force of our circumstances.

Because I didn't know any better or why this was even happening, I felt like the betrayal by those who should have ensured our welfare left a bitter taste in my young heart, reshaping my understanding of authority and fairness. Watching our lives unravel before my eyes, I clenched my fists and whispered a desperate plea, "God, why is this happening? Don't you see what they're doing to us? Please, change this. We can't take much more." My voice quivered as I continued, "You promised to protect us. Please, show us your mercy."

Among my sadness, a passage from Psalms came to mind: "The Lord is close to the brokenhearted and saves those who are crushed in spirit." (Psalm 34:18, NIV). In that moment, those words were a lifeline. I clung to them, whispering, "God, be near us. Deliver us from this nightmare. Restore our home." Each word was an urgent plea, a cry for intervention in a situation that felt beyond repair.

Despite the turmoil around me, I found a fragile sense of peace as I poured my heart into prayer. All I could cling to was that unsteady peace. I believed that God would step in to heal our fractured lives. But as days turned into weeks and weeks stretched into months, and our struggles persisted, doubt began to creep into my faith. Why were my prayers met with silence? Why did our misery persist in spite of my passionate calls?

After the eviction, my family was scattered among relatives, marking a turning point in our lives. My brothers and I found temporary refuge in my grandmother's home, navigating the environment while longing for the unity and comfort of our own family under one roof. It was a time of profound uncertainty and loneliness.

During those months, my mother worked tirelessly to rebuild our lives. She juggled multiple jobs, sought assistance from social agencies, and slowly began piecing our shattered world back together. Her resilience and determination were unwavering, yet it was also a period of immense hardship. As the seventh child of fifteen, I found myself stepping into responsibilities beyond my years, striving to support my siblings emotionally while grappling with my own fears and insecurities.

Through this experience, I learned that faith is not always about immediate answers or miraculous interventions. It is about endurance, resilience, and the quiet strength to face adversity. My faith evolved from expecting instant solutions to embracing a journey of trust and perseverance. I came to understand that God's timing and plans often differ from my own. This transformative period reshaped my understanding of faith and resilience, laying a foundation that would guide me through future challenges.

Looking back, the eviction was more than a loss of shelter; it was the moment my perception of the world changed forever. It taught me the fragility of stability and the enduring strength of hope. Though it was a painful chapter, it became a cornerstone of my journey, shaping the person I would become and igniting a determination to create a life of security and purpose for my own family I had created.

One evening, I recall my older brother sitting next to me, his normally easygoing manner giving way to a serious determination. Even though his voice broke with uncertainty, he added, "We'll get through this." Even though they were brief, his comments gave me hope.

"Ebony," he said, looking at the floor as if the words were difficult. "This cannot be allowed to happen anymore. Not to Momma. Not to us.

I nodded and said, "I know," my own tears streaming down my cheeks. She should never again cry like that, in my opinion. I feel as though something inside of me is being broken. As I talked, my voice broke, and I used the back of my hand to wipe my face while attempting to keep myself composed.

His eyes were hazy yet determined as he turned to face me. "We'll make sure she never has to experience this again when we get older. No more evictions, no more landlords. We are going to look after her.

We'll buy her a house," I murmured, sniffling in an attempt to match his resolve. She can claim it as her own. It will never be taken away from her by anyone.

He nodded, his hand resting softly on my shoulder. "Yes. A home for her. We'll do it whatever it takes. Make me a promise.

Even though tears were flowing down my cheeks, I firmly said, "I promise," in a whisper.

I felt a spark of resolve as we sat there for a while, two hurt kids talking and attempting to bear the weight of a world too huge for us. Our common resolve, which bound us to a future we could build, no matter how unattainable it appeared at the time, felt like a lifeline even in the heart of the disaster.

Like a hurricane, eviction had torn through our family, sending us all in different directions and leaving the debris of our innocence in its wake. It made us face the fragile nature of stability and exposed us to the harsh reality of what it means to lose everything. Nevertheless, we discovered a firm resolve to rebuild and fight for a future free from such tragedy during that storm. I learned a valuable lesson from the experience: nothing worthwhile comes easily, and rebuilding requires resilient behaviors, courage, and an unapologetic will. It was a sign of victory when we were all together in a house, we could call our own, and it was more than just a house with four walls and a roof.

After months of praying and searching, my mother eventually got us a home. Although it wasn't particularly fancy, it belonged to us. We were eager to make a new beginning when we moved in. The rooms were filled with the scent of freshness, and there appeared to be something better around every corner. Eager to make it feel like home, we giggled as we unpacked. As me and my siblings climbed up and down, the brand-new bunk beds creaked under our weight. Naturally, I heard my brothers who were arguing over who should get the top bunk in their room. Each room had a set of comforters, sheets that were the same color as the curtains, and dressers that we stocked with new clothes, socks, and underwear.

We pulled out the new video game console in the boys' room and competed for hours, our voices blending in a clamor of friendly conversation and lighthearted battling. It was the kind of noise, full of life and love, that I had been waiting for—our noise. We were genuinely together for the first time in a long time, and every tiny element of our new place felt like a triumph. We had a house, full of comfort, laughter, and the kind of joy that only siblings can experience, and the days of hardship were over for now.

Chapter 4
A Hard Knock Life

My mother had the ability to transform a wounded heart into a source of hope, a dark room into a haven, and an empty pantry into a feast. Her hands were rough from the many hours she spent working and balancing several jobs, yet she slaved hard. Her days lasted long after the moon rose high in the night sky, and they started before the sun even touched the horizon. I can still picture her today, standing in the kitchen with her back a little bent from fatigue, trying to figure out how to stretch one income to pay for groceries, electricity, rent, and her kids' needs.

Rent, electricity, water, and food all appeared to have names already attached to every dollar she made. She would repeatedly juggle the numbers when there wasn't enough to go around, which was rarely the case, and rob Peter in order to pay Paul in the hopes that Paul wouldn't call and demand payment before Peter received his share.

She never allowed her troubles to become ours, even if they were weighing her down. She would prepare dinners that gave us the impression that we were feasting like kings and queens, even when the refrigerator was almost empty. She would light candles when the lights were out, which gave the night an aura of magic. She made sure we wore clothes that we or she had hand-washed or went to the laundry to wash and excellent shoes that she could afford, and she made sure we went to school with our heads held high. Her voice carried strength even when her body was exhausted.

I want to tell any mothers who have ever felt unnoticed or who have worked themselves to the bone only to believe that it wasn't enough that it did matter. My mother's sacrifices were significant. To her kids, she was a lighthouse that helped us navigate the storm, even if she might have felt like she was treading water in an endless ocean of bills. She claimed that each little triumph—keeping the lights on for another week, figuring out how to pay the rent, and getting us to school on time—was evidence of her hard work and an act of love so deep that words cannot express how it feels.

She taught me that resilience is about getting back up after being knocked down by life, not about never falling. Love, she told me, is in the little things, in the work, in the will to persevere in the face of overwhelming difficulties. Her battle was not in vain; rather, it served as the cornerstone for my own tenacity and resolve.

I can still clearly recall the day I thought the faucet stopped producing the constant flow of water I had become accustomed to and instead sputtered and coughed, generating a weak give of air. I initially believed it to be a brief interruption; perhaps the city was fixing the pipes. But as the hours went by, we realized that the water had been turned off.

As I stared at the dry sink in the bathroom, I yelled out, "Momma, there's no water." Looking over my shoulder, one of my siblings asked, "What are we supposed to do now?"

My mother's expression stiffened, a brief moment of remorse and frustration flashing across her face before she swiftly covered it up with a fake serenity. Her eyes showed the fury raging inside, but her voice remained steady as she added, "Don't worry, I'll figure it out, it'll be back on soon."

My siblings and I collected whatever container we could find that evening, including juice bottles and old milk jugs, and we set out in the dark. The park a few blocks away was our first destination. When we pressed the handle, a tiny stream of water eventually flowed out of the rusted fountain, which moaned. The cold metal bit our palms as my siblings and I alternated filling the jugs.

While looking over her shoulder, Momma said, "Be careful." At the time, I could understand why she didn't want people to see us. It just seemed like a humiliating experience to me. It wasn't until I saw the strain in my siblings' shoulders and how they were constantly looking around the dimly lit park for strangers or our neighborhood friends.

On other evenings, we would sneak onto the neighbor's side yard when we couldn't use the park fountain. We would kneel low in the shadows, holding our breath as we cranked the handle as silently as we could, their outside hose barely disguised. My heart would race in my chest in fear that someone would catch us, and the sound of the running water was loud in the stillness.

To my younger brother, who was having trouble carrying a full jug back to the house, I whispered, "Don't spill it." "I'm not!" he shouted back, swaying from the strain.

It was a tiring but necessary routine at home. We heated the water in big pots on the stove until it was appropriate for short baths or dishwashing. We would line up and take turns using the valuable water we had so diligently gathered for baths. My sister would cry, "Hurry up!" and beat on the restroom door. "My hot water is almost ready!"

We had to gently tilt a jug to wet our toothbrushes and rinse our mouths while brushing our teeth, sparing every drop.

Every once-easy task now needed preparation and work, but we managed to make it work.

I didn't completely understand the gravity of what we were doing as kids. I believed it to be a brief setback that we would later laugh about, just another odd aspect of life. However, looking back, I can see the toll it had on my mother—the way she shook when we turned the spigot, the way she struggled to maintain her composure while telling us that everything would be alright.

She managed to make us feel normal even when we were struggling. As we carried the jugs, she entertained us with anecdotes that helped us forget about the gravity of the situation and the weight of the water. By demonstrating through her actions rather than words that no obstacle was impossible to overcome, she transformed adversity into resilience.

I learned the importance of resourcefulness and the perseverance required to keep going when it seems like the chances were stacked against me from those evenings. It taught me that we were supporting one another throughout the most trying times, not just when it came to carrying water.

We were unprepared when our lights had been cut off for the first time. The beautiful twilight glow filled the home for a minute, and then we were engulfed in a dense blackness. As my smaller siblings wailed in little, terrified tones, I stood there, not knowing what to do.

My mother's voice popped like an indicator through the confusion, "Don't be afraid." With a match that blazed briefly before giving way to a tiny, flickering flame, she lit a few of the emergency candles kept in the drawer. Her face was lit by the golden light, and despite her composed demeanor, the worry she had worked so hard to protect us from was there in her eyes.

We were crowded together like campers around a fire in the living room that night. According to Momma, it was only a brief setback, like a passing storm. However, we had to adjust when the days became into weeks.

The first obstacle was the refrigerator. The food we depended on began to deteriorate without electricity. Momma came up with a clever solution: she packed a cooler full of ice and the necessities—milk, eggs, and a few other perishables—tightly within. Her hands were cold and red from carrying the large bags, so every day she or we would walk to the corner store to buy more ice.

She looked for another route when that became costly enough. She borrowed an extension cord one evening after talking to a neighbor. We extended it from their outdoor outlet into our home as it was becoming dark. It was a minor triumph in a sea of difficulties, barely enough to keep the refrigerator running.

She told me to "hold it steady" as I untangled the lengthy orange cord. Together, my siblings and I plugged it into the refrigerator after putting it through the screen door or the kitchen window. The room echoed with a collective sigh of relief as soon as we heard the motor's familiar hum. Half to herself, she whispered, "At least we won't lose the food."

41

We discovered new methods to connect when there was no light. We started having candlelit meals every night, where we would sit close to each other and giggle while the shadows danced on the walls. Because there was no power, we had to rely on one another for comfort and enjoyment, and board games took the role of television.

During a Monopoly game, my sister would shove the dice in my direction and remark, "Your turn." When someone eventually found themselves on Boardwalk, owing rent they couldn't afford, the crowd would burst into laughter.

Momma stayed our rock through it all. Even when our circumstances weren't amusing, she made sure we found the humor in them. She transformed what may have been depressing moments into lessons about perseverance. She would remind us that we were stronger than this. And for some reason, we trusted her.

Connection was more important than survival during these times in the dark. We supported one another, gained knowledge from one another, and discovered strength in our connection. Even though the lights were muted by the absence of electricity, it highlighted the ties of love and tenacity that bound us all together.

In looking back, those evenings showed me that, if you chose to make it, there can be light even in the darkest moments. We not only made it through the dark, but we excelled there, and the lessons I took away still serve as a guide for me today.

I put on such a convincing mask at school that nobody could have suspected the difficulties I faced at home. As though my life wasn't falling apart behind closed doors, I smiled broadly as I strolled down the hallways, enthusiastically greeted teachers, and joked with friends. A girl who excelled on tests, engaged in class discussions, and made jokes in the lunchroom was spotted by my classmates. They missed the girl who ate dinner by candlelight because the electricity had been turned off—again—or who spent her mornings snatching water from a neighbor's spigot.

I was taught early on how to erect a stronghold and invisible wall around my inner world. I turned school into a haven where I could act as though nothing was wrong. I did well in the classroom because it was something I could manage, not because I sought praise. During a lesson, I would use the work at hand as a diversion when my stomach rumbled. When I was invited to a friend's house for an overnight stay, I would excuse myself by saying that I couldn't accept the offer or that I didn't have clean clothing to bring.

A close friend once inquired, her expression confused, "Why don't you ever want to hang out, ever?" I forced a laugh and shrugged. I said, "Just busy with family stuff," hoping she wouldn't ask any more questions.

I felt both protected and burdened by that façade of normalcy. I was shielded from criticism, but I had to bear my suffering by myself. I didn't want sympathy or inquiries to which I couldn't respond. Rather, I focused my efforts on demonstrating that I was capable of overcoming my situation.

I told myself every morning when I entered the school that my difficulties did not define who I was. They weren't the whole narrative; they were just the background. I resolutely and tenaciously fortified myself, building an inner fortress brick by brick.

"You are more than this," I carried Gram's voice inside that castle. Her words stuck in my head during the most trying times and became my inspiration. I always reminded myself that this was just temporary whenever I felt the weight of it all, whether I was sitting in class pretending not to hear my hunger grumble or avoiding questions about what I was doing over the weekend.

Small triumphs, like a perfect test score, a teacher's praise, or a chuckle with a friend, also gave me courage. I was reminded that better times were ahead by these moments, which were like rays of sunshine penetrating my stronghold.

In addition to being a performance, school served as a testing ground. It demonstrated to me my greater potential than I had previously thought. I learned how to rise above life's attempts to drag me down.

Upon reflection, I see that those times were not just about getting by, but also about developing the fortitude that would enable me to overcome any obstacle life presented. Although my mask concealed my difficulties, it also gave me the opportunity to shine in ways I never would have imagined. And through it all, I discovered that being strong is about making the decision to keep moving forward, one step at a time, rather than trying to hide your suffering.

Unquestionably, we had to deal with days of uncertainty, evenings without power, and nights spent carrying water. However, those struggles gave me priceless insights into fortitude, resourcefulness, and thankfulness. I discovered how to cherish each tiny blessing and make the most of what little we had. Most significantly, I discovered the value of empathy—knowing what it's like to struggle and wishing to relieve others of that weight.

My mother's devotion remained unwavering throughout everything. Our survival was based on her sacrifices, and I was inspired by her strength. She demonstrated to me what it meant to stand up for your family in the face of overwhelming obstacles.

My desire to work as a social worker was stoked by these encounters. I want to be the one to help people going through difficult times as we experienced by offering empathy, resources, and helpful advice. I keep those lessons in mind as I work to positively influence people who, like me, feel invisible and unheard.

The purpose of life's challenges is to build resilience and character, not to shatter us. Every obstacle I encountered, such as bringing water in the middle of the night or locating light during my darkest moments, taught me the value of tenacity. Every challenge made me more determined and served as a reminder that there is always a lesson to be learned, even in the most trying circumstances.

I have developed a strong empathy for other people as a result of these encounters. I understand what it's like to smile through suffering, carrying a weight in silent, and to wish someone could relate. This knowledge is what motivates me to help people recognize their strengths and overcome obstacles.

Remember this for anyone going through their own struggles: your situation does not define you; rather, it sets you up for success. Even while the path may be difficult, it is making you stronger, wiser, and more competent than you ever imagined. Keep going, even if you fail to recognize your own strength.

Chapter 5

Trading Fear for Hustle: My Sister's Legacy

My sister was the type of person that didn't let our situation define who we were. Armed with resolve and a strategy, she woke my brother and I up at the crack of dawn one summer morning. She had made the decision that we would earn our own money. This event was the start of a journey that would educate me how to invest in my future and myself in addition to how to hustle.

Opportunities seemed limited and problems were ongoing in the South Louisville community where my siblings and I grew up, which was close to Churchill Downs. My sister took matters into her own hands after growing weary of seeing our mother struggle to make ends meet. She showed us that we could create our own possibilities rather than waiting for someone to give us a break.

It all began with an elderly woman who lived on Denmark, directly across the street from our home. She was our very first customer. We started raking leaves, shoveling snow, and cutting grass with the equipment our mother had purchased to keep our yard in good condition. Word of our diligence quickly spread, and we attracted more customers.

Everything was planned by my sister. She made sure that we changed out of our school uniforms as soon as possible so that we could go to work. Our customers learned to trust us and waited for us on the days we were scheduled because she instilled in each of us the values of discipline and dependability. Not everyone was nice; we had to cope with unpleasant, racist people as well as rejection. However, that didn't discourage us. Our motivation came from the delight of helping our mother with expenses and household necessities.

I learned about reinvestment from her as well and didn't even know it. Even though I wasn't in high school yet, I recall gathering money for the Moore High School choir while I was outside the Southland Terrace shopping center. Later, she showed me how to double or even triple my earnings by using the money I worked hard for to buy snacks and resale them. My earliest lessons in self-investment and entrepreneurship came from those experiences.

My sister continued to mentor me as I got older. Going into high school, she helped me land my first job at Wendy's. I frequently snapped at work because I was frustrated with our living circumstances, not realizing how it affected her. She never stopped believing in me. Every time I gave up, she urged me to get back up stronger.

After Wendy's, I worked at a number of different jobs before she helped me land a job with the USPS. After eight hard years of employment, the demanding schedule and lack of family time made me reevaluate my career path. I eventually made the switch to a position in corrections after realizing that I would never be able to achieve the freedom I desired while working for others. At the point of losing that job, I made the decision to invest in myself by becoming a speaker and a catalyst for change.

Looking back, I can see how I was influenced by my sister's example. She taught me to turn fear into motivation for my hustling and to embrace the pain and discomfort that comes with hard work. Her perseverance demonstrated to me that our circumstances have the power to either teach or break us. She gave me the motivation to go beyond my comfort zone, create a life where I could have an impact, and make uncomfortable my new normal.

The values my sister taught were me—resilience, resourcefulness, and the guts to take chances—that live on the inside me. My life is braided with her influence, and I apply her teachings to all I do. She was and will continue to be my inspiration.

At one point in my life, when I was having a hard time believing in myself, I couldn't comprehend why another of my sisters loved me so much. She was my foundation of strength and a symbol of hope when things got tough. She taught me the value of self-care and self-love, which at the time I wasn't even aware I needed. This is where I discuss her constant presence and how she helped me learn to accept who I am.

I had difficulties as a child that made me feel alone and misinterpreted. I had a hard time believing that I was worthy of love or respect because of my past experiences. My confidence was undermined by numerous family members who made fun of me by calling me names like "little boy" or "dikes." But I was never criticized by my sister. She saw the fragile young girl behind the protective shell and understood the anguish I carried from my past. She provided me with the confidence that I wasn't alone and the room to articulate how I felt.

She showed me more than words could express. When I had my first child, she stepped in to make sure he had everything he needed and more. She provided for me in ways that I was unable to provide for myself or give back to her. She became my go-to person for everything from getting my hair done for school to making sure I had clothes for every event.

My eighth-grade graduation was one of the most unforgettable evenings of my life. I was devastated since my mother said she was not going to my big event or even cared that I required clothes for it. The sorrow of her absence was too great for me to bear; therefore, I didn't want to leave. My sister and her closest friend wouldn't let me skip the event by staying at home. They both reminded me that this was my accomplishment and that no one, not even my parents, could take it away from me with unwavering love and resolve. I was able to celebrate myself that evening because of their remarks.

She has been my pillar of support at every turn in my life. She demonstrated unconditional love for me by teaching me self-care skills and me a shoulder to cry on. She supported me in confronting my challenges and worries instead of ignoring them. She taught me how to present myself confidently, even when I felt worthless, with everything from hairstyles to makeup.

More significantly, she had a deeper understanding of me than anyone else. We talked endlessly about how I didn't want to dress in a way that would draw attention from males who would take advantage of my innocence. She encouraged me to accept my natural appearance rather than pressuring me to be someone I wasn't. Her assistance helped me to strike a balance between recovering my identity as a young lady and paying respect to my past.

When I think back on her influence, I realize how much of my resiliency stems from her steadfast love and encouragement. She taught me to take pride in who I am, even when others don't. She taught me that my worth is based on how much I love and care for myself, not on what other people think.

My sister is a source of strength and optimism, not just a role model. Her legacy endures in the self-worth lessons she taught me and the confidence she gave me. I still look to her for advice, and her love has shaped me into the woman I am today.

Sharing this chapter required openness and vulnerability because they show the transformational power of unconditional love, how to work hard to achieve your goals, and empathy for others who feel invisible or undeserving. For those who might have had comparable difficulties, my story serves as evidence of the resilience that arises from being completely understood and encouraged by someone who never gives up on you. It is my goal to demonstrate to others that they are not alone and that their suffering does not define them; rather, it can strengthen their courage and progress by sharing these really personal experiences.

This attitude of working hard to accomplish what is required while placing a high value on confidence and self-care will continue to be crucial as I reflect on my path as a future social worker. I've learned from these experiences that vulnerability and the guts to stand up for oneself and others are often necessary for thriving. I was inspired to believe that no matter where you come from or what you've been through, you can overcome it by my sister's unfailing support. This conviction will direct me as I help others overcome their own obstacles and find their inner strength.

# Chapter 6

Silent No More

Long shadows are thrown against the walls by the mellow light from a single floor lamp in the poorly lighted space. The middle is filled with a circle of mismatched chairs, each inhabited by a person whose face is inscribed with a story. The muffled buzz of pre-session whispering fades as the therapist, a calm woman with compassionate eyes, slowly clears her throat, and the air hums with a mixture of tension and quiet expectancy. The clean perfume of the room is mixed with the faint aroma of coffee that has been prepared at a corner table.

My fingers are intertwined and lying on my lap as I sit close to the window. My heart is thumping in my ears, so even when the therapist introduces herself, I hardly hear her. The strangers surrounding me nod courteously to each other, their gazes flitting from face to face. A woman tightens the edge of her scarf, a man nervously bounces his knee, and another woman looks at the floor as though she's looking for answers in the old carpet.

It was different today. The weight of my choice weighs heavily on my chest. I was here to share my truth, the secret that has been kept for years like a scar.

Why now? I pondered. My chest constricted as the question replayed itself in my head. However, I already knew the answer in my heart. If I ever wanted to feel free again, I couldn't keep suppressing it.

The therapist broke through my swirling thoughts with a welcoming smile.

With a firm yet friendly tone, she opened by saying, "Thank you all for being here today." Sharing, listening, and healing are all welcome in this area. Here, there is only support—no judgment. Who wants to get started?

After that, there was a long, heavy pause as everyone looked at each other hesitantly. A middle-aged woman to my right finally raised her voice. As she told a story of treachery, her voice faltered, her words unvarnished, shaky, and courageous. I felt a tiny spark of connection and found myself nodding a little. At the same time, though, I started to feel anxious.

After she was done, everyone started talking. Others expressed their feelings in a deluge of words, while others provided brief, broken sentences. A part of me was in awe of their bravery as I listened carefully. The therapist then faced me.

"You haven't spoken," she remarked softly. "Are you willing to share?"

I could feel my heart pounding and my throat getting dry. I looked around the circle and saw faces that were either inscrutable or sympathetic. I nodded, taking a long breath.

"I... "I suppose I should begin at the beginning," I said, scarcely raising my voice above a whisper. It's difficult to discuss. I've had the feeling for a long time that saying it aloud would make it real.

The therapist gave a supportive nod. "Take your time."

I grounded myself by holding onto the edges of my chair. I started by saying, "Something happened when I was younger—something I didn't understand at the time." Besides... Since then, I've kept it close at hand. My self-perception and my level of trust in others have been greatly influenced by it.

A man leaned forward a little on the other side of the circle. "I understand that sensation," he uttered quietly. "Like it's in the back of your mind all the time."

I looked him in the eye and smiled slightly, appreciatively. "Exactly," I said. However, I'm sick of it ruling me. I am here for that reason. Even if it sounds crazy, I simply need to let it out.

Once more, the therapist spoke softly. By telling us about this, you're showing courage. Also, keep in mind that you don't have to say everything at once. The process of healing is a process.

With a harder voice, I nodded. "I'm grateful. I believe it's been a while since I've seen a safe space like this.

As the session went on, I noticed a slight but noticeable change within myself—a glimmer of light where there had before been just darkness. The weight felt somewhat less heavy for the first time in years. Even though it was uncertain, the way forward appeared somewhat more obvious.

After taking a long breath, I realized that I had to eventually speak up at that silent time. At first, my voice wavered, but as the words came out, I was able to understand each one clearly. The truth that had long been hidden within of me was now clamoring to be heard.

"I... I guess I have to tell everything," I said, the words weighing heavily on my shoulders. "The experiences that molded me and the ones that caused me pain." Although it's difficult, I can no longer hold it in anymore.

For a few seconds, I allowed the silence to linger, as though I needed to gather my strength before venturing into the darkness of my past. Then, with a silent determination, I began to reveal my story I had long suppressed.

61

"I didn't comprehend what was going on when I was younger. It was just a part of my existence, and I had no idea how to label the agony or the terror. Of course, there were happy times, but they were always overshadowed by the things that were beyond my control. I can recall the first time. Then became really afraid to speak my story. I paused the said "I was a baby, no more than two years of age." The second time, I was only a young child, maybe five or six years old. In an instant, my sense of security was destroyed. It seems as though everything that ought to have been cozy and reassuring—the trust, the love, and the protection—was abruptly torn away."

The room felt like it was closing in on me, so I stopped and swallowed hard. At my sides, my fingers balled into fists.

I recall hearing accusations that I was to blame because I was very sensitive. I carried the hurt and the rage even if they weren't mine. That is not how a child should ever feel—trapped in a place that ought to have been a safe place, made to grow up in ways that no one should. I was unaware at the time and even afraid to tell adults, but I later learn that my innocence had been taken from me.

The confusion only became worse as I entered my adolescent years. The harassment persisted, but it took on a new appearance. In many respects, I was still a child even though I had matured. The game's rules remained the same, but it felt like the world around me had transformed. I became a part of the silence and the shame.

I attempted to make sense of things during my adolescence, but all I managed to do was get more lost. I became adept at closing down and hiding behind walls of silence. I kept convincing myself that it wasn't real, that I could disregard the words and scars, the painful moments that followed me everywhere. However, they consistently returned. The quiet grew louder. I didn't even know how to explain what had happened without feeling like I was solely to blame, let alone how to seek for help. "This isn't right," was something I couldn't even articulate."

I shakily exhaled as the memories of being forgotten and invisible swirled around me.

However, the silence that surrounding the abuse was worse than the actual torture itself. I felt like no one would believe me, so I wanted to shout and tell someone. I thought no one was interested enough to pay attention. It all added to the disbelief and self-doubt. I began to think I was to blame and that I wasn't deserving of anything better.

Then came early adulthood, when I believed I would be able to move on from my past. However, the patterns—those ingrained pain patterns—followed me.

I believed that I could outrun it. I believed that all of the things that had plagued me for so long would be gone once I reached adulthood. However, I was actually still holding them. The abuse had influenced my self-perception and my level of trust—or lack thereof—in other people. Years passed before I understood that what I was repeating wasn't typical. that I shouldn't simply "move past" what I had gone through.

I spoke more steadily as I leaned forward. When I eventually began to see the trends, I was in my twenties. I ended up in relationships that were similar to what I had experienced as a child. At first, I was blind to the falsehoods, the control, and the manipulation. I started to resist, though, gently. I resisted the pattern, telling myself that I was deserving of better and that I didn't need to continue allowing the past to dictate my present. However, that battle was tiring. I also lost occasionally.

Adulthood was the last straw, a lie that destroyed everything I had worked so hard to achieve.

I believed that I had at last found stability and that the storm had passed when I was in my late twenties. I had created a sense of purpose, a career, and relationships that made me feel protected. But in a single act of lying, it was all destroyed. This individual, whom I believed to be my coworker, abandoned me, which was the last thing I ever expected to happen. Everything I had worked for seemed to be slipping away from me in an instant.

With a sharp exhale, I clasped my palms together, my hands shaking. It served as my last reminder that the wounds from my past still existed. The agony I believed I had buried deep within of me came back to haunt me. I lost everything because of that betrayal, including the connections I had fostered and the trust I had finally gained in myself. I began to wonder if everything I had worked for had been genuine or if it was all a flimsy delusion.

I hesitated as the words' weight fell upon me like a sorrowful blanket.

However, I came to the realization that it was time to come out of hiding during that period of grief. I have to quit allowing the past to dictate my future. Also, it is possible that this truth—this painful and hurtful truth—was the first step toward discovering the true me that I had nearly forgotten.

I inhaled deeply once more as I felt the room's silence descend upon me. My background was no longer a secret, but it still carried a tremendous burden. And perhaps—just possibly—that marked the start of recovery.

The words weighed heavily and relentlessly on my chest as I related these fragments of my past. I was reliving more than just the memories; I was also reliving the years of silence, the constant stress of bearing them alone, and the anxiety of being seen. I felt like I was removing a layer of protection I had worked so hard to create with every phrase. I had a tsunami surge of emotions as I talked, including rage, anguish, guilt, and even relief. It was a rush, a rush of suddenly feeling everything I had long suppressed. A silent, fading hope was another thing, though. I felt for the first time that I might be able to break free from their hold on me. Knowing that I had finally spoken up for the truth that had been suppressed for so long brought a weird sense of serenity, even though the road ahead was unknown.

A thick silence, the kind that feels more oppressive than calm, lingered in the air after I had finished expressing my truth. Knowing that this would be the most difficult moment of all, I turned to face my family. Their expressions, the ones who had witnessed my development, were now a mix of discomfort and incredulity. Some completely avoided looking at me, instead focusing on the ceiling or the floor. Others furrowed their brows at me, as though they were attempting to make sense of the person I had just described and the person they believed they knew. They were silently accusing me of making it all up and embellishing the past, and I could feel the weight of their judgment in the room.

Then the words came. Sharp and cruel, they cut through the air like knives. My mother remarked in a tense voice, "That never happened." "You're telling lies." The person who should have been my protector now questioned what I had just said, and her comments struck me like a blow to the chest. She seemed to be attempting to hide the truth from herself by denying what had happened and erasing the sorrow. As she talked, my pulse raced, and for a little instant, I experienced that old, well-known sense of shame, as though her incredulity somehow diminished the validity of what I had to say.

Family members who understood the grief I had carried for so long, however, raised their voices in support of me even in the middle of the storm. In a low but forceful voice, a family member who had always listened to me spoke up on a phone call. Her voice was firm and steady as she stated, "You're telling the truth." "I've witnessed what you've been trying to say for years. I can tell you're telling the truth because I can feel the pain you are carrying in voice.

In the sea of cynicism, her comments were a ray of hope, a tiny light in the darkness. One of my cousins, another family member, agreed. She said quietly, "You've always tried to tell me." "They simply didn't want to hear it or counting your truth out."

Their belief in me helped me fight back against the charges, and their support was a lifeline when I felt like I was drowning. It was a beginning, but it wasn't enough to make up for the anguish of having people who ought to have supported me labeling me a liar. And I came to the crucial realization that, despite the fact that some people couldn't or wouldn't see it, my truth mattered. I wasn't alone myself.

It occurred over the telephone. I had hoped that the conversation would lead to some understanding, but it soon turned into a verbal battleground. Hearing my mother's piercing, irate voice made my heart accelerate. "You have no idea what you're talking about," she responded, sounding defensive and accusatory. "How dare you act like this, dragging names through the mud? What's the matter with you? It wasn't the right time or place to bring that up, and now you've destroyed someone else day.

Each of her comments struck more deeply than the last, forming a blur of betrayal. Yes, I have heard her like this before—her emotions unrestrained and raw, her voice shaking with rage. She didn't want to hear my side of the story and wouldn't even let me explain. Rather, she launched an assault, accusing me of destroying the reputation of a family member that I had once frantically attempted to defend.

She eventually spat, the hatred in her words almost choking, "You're dead to me." "I wish I hadn't had ya. You cannot lie in such a way and expect me to want ya in my life.

My heart sank into the pit of my stomach as if the floor had collapsed beneath me. It stung as the words echoed through the space between us, striking me like a slap. I was told by my mother that I was dead. I wanted to yell and plead with her to comprehend, but I knew that would not make a difference. And she was going to turn away.

For a minute, I was gripped by the pain of her rejection, which wrapped around me like a smothering blanket. Then, though, something changed within me. Unbeknownst to me, I experienced a burst of strength that propelled me to confront her poison. I said, "My peace is your peace," with a composure that even startled me, allowing the words to sink into the silence between us. I stopped, inhaled deeply, and then went on. However, I can no longer bear your rage. I must let go.

Then I hung up without waiting for a reply. I couldn't dispute the finality of the phone click that echoed in my ears.

The immediate aftermath was a whirlwind of feelings, including uncertainty, anger, and loss. I wanted to break down and cry, but I refrained. Instead, I felt a strange sense of relief and emptiness as I stood there and stared at the phone in my palm. It was like losing a piece of who I was, a part of my identity that I had held onto for so long, when I lost her love and support. However, I came to the crucial realization that I could no longer allow my desire for her acceptance to control my life.

The loss of my mother's support seemed like a raw wound that would take time to heal; the pain was genuine. However, I was aware that by cutting that connection, I had allowed myself to be true to who I am. I would defend myself at all costs. And as I worked through the fallout from that discussion, I realized that sometimes standing up for what you believe in involves losing what you considered important. However, it also means obtaining your own peace, which is considerably more significant.

It wasn't simple to process the pain. For days, I felt as like I was drowning in sadness, rage, and a debilitating loneliness that would eventually consume me. The absence of my mother's affection was like a raw, broad hole in my chest. I was upset with myself for even wanting her acceptance after everything, and I cried when I felt like I couldn't. On other nights, though, I just sat quietly and allowed the weight of everything to hang on me because I knew that in order to recover, I had to feel it. The rage that she was willing to cut up relationships so readily and that she was unable to recognize my truth also bubbled up. Every feeling collided with every other one, leaving me worn out yet unbroken.

I had brief epiphanies in the middle of that storm. I started to unearth a strength that had always existed but had been long hidden. Even when it seemed like everything was crumbling around me, I was able to remind myself of my value in the small murmurs to myself. "I am sufficient. Even if it weren't always easy to say, I would reiterate, "My voice matters." I gradually came to see that my truth was not only for myself, but also for everyone who had been silenced and who needed to hear that it was always okay to speak up for what you believe in, no matter the cost.

I developed resilience in the face of suffering. It was about going on despite the pain, not about avoiding it. I started to realize that my value was independent of other people's opinions. I was stronger than I had ever been because I was able to stand by my convictions even when I was rejected. Even though the trip was lengthy, and the pain persisted, every day served as a reminder that I was taking back my strength, my voice, and my peace.

My motivation comes from transforming my suffering into a purpose. Regaining my power seemed to begin with enrolling in a social work school. I wanted to use the hurt, rage, and loneliness I had gone through to do something worthwhile, like advocate for those who were as voiceless as I had been. Every class and project serve as a reminder that, despite its hardships, my journey had a reason. In addition to healing myself, I was getting ready to give others the voice that had been denied to me for so long and to assist them in finding their strength.

When I look back, I can see how every event—every hardship and every triumph—has influenced the job I perform today. My tenacity is demonstrated by the stories I hear and every individual I assist. It serves as a reminder that there is always hope and a purpose to press on, even in the darkest of circumstances. And I'm leaving a legacy with each individual I help along the way—one based on compassion, fortitude, and the unwavering conviction that everyone should be heard.

I'm no longer silent! That straightforward fact has turned into my anthem and my proclamation to both the outside world and to myself. No matter how much fear tries to quiet me or how much my voice trembles, I will never again let myself be silenced.

I want everyone who reads this to know that they are worthy of being heard, even if they feel like their voice is unimportant. Even when it feels too weighty to speak, your truth has strength. Despite your doubts, find that voice, cling to it, and allow it to speak. I see a journey where activism and speaking the truth are not only a mission but a lifetime commitment, one that is lighted by optimism and tenacity. I will continue Encouraging Minds, speaking, and fighting for those who are still silenced, I promise to myself and to anybody who needs to know they are not alone.

Chapter 7

Unraveled Bonds

There's a peace that lasts beyond time, in the middle of life's peaceful moments, in the smell of cooking, hearing it sizzling and the sound of laughter. I can still clearly picture the magical sight that came to life that sunny morning, with the air filled with the aroma of tantalizing food and wisps of smoke dancing off the grill. A picture of contented unity was created by the family's embrace and their laughing mingling with the soft wind. Even so, there is a sharp contrast to this happy recollection of a story that has been upended because it was against this perfect background that Child Protective Services (CPS) loomed large, permanently changing the course of my life.

With the fading light of dusk covering the remains of a productive day, our once lively assembly shrank to a close-knit family circle. After most of the family left, the peaceful evening spread out and relied on my brother, his friend, my ex, my kids, and me. Though the day had been filled with small pleasures and laughter with friends, and family, there was a hint of anxiety as night approached. The loud music interrupted the peaceful atmosphere of our home as I held the baby in my arms. It was an unwanted disturbance to the serene haven of our nightly routines. Encouraged by the good vibes of the evening, my ex-husband continued to party despite my requests for a break. My tolerance was being chewed up by exhaustion and frustration, a silent cry for peace in the middle of chaos. Thus, in the discordant symphony, I was at conflict with the night and yearned for the comfort of sleep while my tired kids curled up in their beds, blind to the chaos all around them.

    It was just an ordinary evening, but the air was heavy with the lingering stench of alcohol and the discordant notes of music booming at an excruciating volume. My ex seemed to be oblivious to the passing of time in his intoxicated perplexity, partying nonstop into the night with an irrational determination. Amidst the pandemonium, there was a fleeting moment of clarity when my brother's friend urgently screamed out for my husband. It was only when he emerged from the restroom, a shadowy figure, that I realized where he was.

The noise of the evening built to a climax while I busied myself in the kitchen making the baby a bottle, broken only by brief bursts of dialogue that broke through the fog of intoxicated bewilderment. I remained motionless, a mute observer of the night's brittle calm, caught in the crossfire of questions and accusations. As time went on, the stress increased and turned into a whirlwind of feelings as my ex, overcome with rage and drunkenness, let out a barrage of hate that echoed throughout our house. I was holding our baby boy tight when I felt myself on the verge of panic in that terrifying moment. My gut told me to run away from the storm that was raging inside him.

Tensions quickly increased as the evening went on, creating an unsettling atmosphere after the family get-together. My ex and I had a sudden altercation as my brother and his friend were standing on the porch. I begged him to leave in a fit of rage because I could not stand to be in a relationship where there was no respect for each other. But my request simply made him more enraged, launching a barrage of threats and verbal abuse that sent his manner spiraling into a terrifying act of hostility.

In a desperate bid to shield both myself and our infant son from harm, I instinctively attempted to evade his advances, raising a defensive hand as he closed in with alarming velocity. Despite my efforts, the altercation escalated, culminating in a series of blows that left me reeling from the impact, while my child bore the brunt of the violence, his tender head bearing the scars of an encounter wrought with chaos. Determined to safeguard our home from further turmoil, I issued an ultimatum, insisting that he leave the premises, only to be met with defiant resistance as he adamantly asserted his claim to our shared home. I looked to my brother and his friend for help during a desperate moment, but they were nowhere to be found, so I was forced to deal with the upheaval on my own so, I called the police.

After the chaotic night, when the sirens eventually faded and some sort of peace returned to our house, I was left to consider the seriousness of the situation. I headed out on a voyage full of doubt and worry as the adrenaline faded and the weight of the events overwhelmed me. It was crucial for me to alert the authorities, but even as my ex was being led away from our home in the back of a police cruiser to his moms, a dark cloud of fear continued to hover over the shaky calm that had settled over our house.

I was faced with a harsh truth in the peaceful seclusion of the morning as the sun shone down on our cozy residence. It was heartbreaking to see our baby, his pure face tarnished by a noticeable large knot on his sensitive scalp, and to be reminded of the violence that had occurred just hours earlier. I was afraid and desperate, so I turned to the people who were closest to me for support and direction as we faced imminent danger. A web of dishonesty started to take shape with every hushed chat as I struggled with the terrifying idea of navigating a system cloaked in uncertainty and terror.

I was afraid, but I knew I had to do something. My entire attention shifted to protecting my child, a purpose that surpassed all uncertainty and fear. I had to make the tough choice to get in touch with a friend who I had once trusted but had grown distant from—someone who had always talked forcefully about truth and sticking up for what's right.

Their expression hardened as I described what had happened that evening; it was a mixture of fear and determination. "You can't let this slide," they stated in a tough but sympathetic tone. The fact was, though, I had no idea where to start. The system seemed like a complex maze created to keep people like me quiet, scared, and lost.

Every move ahead seemed risky. Fear of punishment and the possibility of scrutiny that could shift the focus from him the abuser to me were associated with filing a report. What if they believed that I couldn't keep my child safe? What if it broke us apart rather than brought us together? I kept thinking about these questions, which made every choice feel like balancing on a tightrope over a cliff.

But I knew there was no other choice as I watched my baby's eyes search mine for love and safety. My love for my child outweighed my fear on the night this happened. I remember

I dialed 911 for assistance with shaking hands, each ring on the other end felt like a countdown to an unknown future.

I hesitated for a moment before forcing out the words, "I need help," when the voice answered. My child was struck in the head.

I experienced a mix of relief and fear at that same instant, like if a dam had burst inside of me. The next discussion was challenging and awkward, with inquiries that came off as more accusations than offers of assistance. However, there was an appeal of hope concealed in the caseworker's cold tone. Someone had paid attention. The intervention process had already begun.

After hanging up, I looked at my child. I was brought back to the present by his tiny hand wrapping around my finger. I muttered, more to persuade myself than to him, "We're going to get through this."

I was determined to fight for a better future—not only for him, but for all of my children—even though I knew the path ahead would be difficult. I gave myself permission to think that there might be hope at the end of this terrifying trip for the first time in a long time.

In the midst of trauma and violence, this chapter "Unraveled Bonds" eloquently illustrates the mismatch between brief moments of happiness and the breakdown of family stability. Many people can identify with the image of a calm family get-together broken up by chaos because it captures the delicate balance between love, discomfort, and the pressing need for safety. This emphasizes the intense emotional upheaval of dealing with the immediate fallout from violence as well as the anxiety of unknowable outcomes. It is a story of perseverance, fortitude, and the agonizing realization that sometimes-facing hard realities is necessary in the name of peace.

We are reminded of the value of speaking up when faced with hardship as I think back on this journey. While sharing my stories might bring about the necessary transformation and healing, silence frequently feeds fear and permits suffering to continue. My story urges us to act, not just to help victims of abuse because we are in a relationship with them, but also to promote policies that safeguard and empower survivors. Each of us can contribute to the creation of safer, more supportive settings for our families, whether it is by lending a sympathetic ear, spreading awareness, or participating in neighborhood initiatives.

Therefore, let's set a challenge for ourselves to end the cycles of fear and violence that threaten the peace that we all deserve. Let this serve as a catalyst for change, inspiring us to create more robust and resilient communities where families are safeguarded, individuals are supported, and the links that bind us together are less likely to break. Action is the first step on the path to peace, and it starts with us.

The power of choice—the kind of choice that determines our identity and the legacy we leave behind—became clear to me after that. Making the decision to have my child means putting love, security, and hope ahead of guilt, fear, and complacency. It meant releasing myself from the silence that had held me back for so long.

I learned from this experience that real strength comes from facing pain head-on rather than putting up with it. It demonstrated to me that love is more than simply an emotion; it is an unrelenting dedication to preserving and fostering what is most important. Most significantly, it served as a reminder that healing starts when we have the courage to change the story and stop allowing the past to control the present.

I promised myself, my other two children, and my infant son that I would create a life based on courage, compassion, and trust as I held him in my arms. In order to give them a childhood full of the peace and safety I never knew, I would make sure that the cycles of violence and fear ended with me.

And to anyone who is at a similar crossroads, know that even when it seems impossible, you have the strength to choose the correct path. Change can be sparked by your bravery, love, and unwillingness to accept anything less than what you and your loved ones deserve. We can work together to build a society in which love always wins out over fear and where every child grows up knowing they are loved, safe, and allowed to dream.

Chapter 8
When CPS Entered Our Lives

The next morning, I kept calling my ex's number out of desperation, but all I got was silence. Hours went by, minutes that seemed to go on forever, as I frantically left voicemails and typed texts. I finally got to his mom. Explaining the urgency of our son's need to visit the hospital and his father's need to be present to provide an explanation for what had happened made my voice quaver. Fear turned around and bit me in that turbulent time, not only for my eight-day old son but also for the possibility of my children being taken, being falsely charged, and imprisoned for something I hadn't done.

My baby was in the backseat, his faint whimpers piercing my soul, and I drove to the hospital in a blur, my pulse racing in my chest the entire way. The emergency room was bustling with sterile lights and hurried people when we got there. I was trying to remember the lies I was told to say by the family members I trusted but, Doctors and nurses rushed to take my son from me, their expressions masking their professional concern.

I was left waiting in the area, and the worst-case possibilities kept running through my head. Before long, a nurse appeared with a clipboard and friendly but perceptive eyes. She wanted me to tell her the whole story. As I attempted to put together a logical story, my words came out stumbling and unfinished. It was not enough, though. A doctor and another nurse arrived, asking the same questions, and going a little further each time.

It felt like hours passed in a haze of unanswered questions before a child protection worker showed up. Her eyes were piercing and unblinking, despite her serene demeanor. After giving a brief introduction, she started asking pointed questions one after the other. Fear surged up like a tidal wave, and I felt the walls closing in around me. Why am I protecting the man that hurt our child? Why not just tell them exactly what happened and not what I was coheres into saying? What if I was not believed by them? What if they believed that I had hurt my son in some way?

My early recollections, my ongoing dread of punishment, and my natural tendency to tell lies to shield myself all came to the surface. I started to falter, answering questions incoherently and blurting out straight lies and half-truths. The fear was too strong for me to control. The worker, and security guard's inquiries became more pointed, their stare sharper, and I realized I was getting deeper and deeper into trouble.

However, the fear of getting in trouble was instilled in me as a survival mechanism from a time when telling the truth was commonly punished. I wanted to shield my son from the imminent consequences, but my old self-preservation tendencies were paralyzing me at that very time. My deception served as both my shield and my downfall.

I could sense doubt and mistrust in the worker's eyes as the questioning went on. I could not escape the routines of my past; I was caught in a web of my own design. It was unbearable to be afraid of losing my children and of being held responsible for something I had not done. And in that terror, I forgot what mattered most: my children needed me to be better, stronger, and honest.

The child protection lady looked directly into my eyes, showing a visible diminishing of her patience. "I'm going to give you one more chance to tell me what happened to this baby," she stated in a calm yet chilly tone. "He has a blood clot above his brain and two fractures to his skull. This was not just a brawl and dispute in a play or an accident." She then left the room, leaving us to deal with the weight of her words and our concerns on our own.

As soon as the door closed, I turned to my ex, my voice a frantic whisper. "We can't keep lying. She knows something's off. We might as well tell the truth about what happened."

He looked at me, his eyes filled with the same fear I felt. "But what if they take him away? What if they think it's your fault?"

"They already suspect us both," I replied, my voice trembling. "If we keep lying, it will only get worse. We need to tell the truth before it's too late."

He hesitated for a moment, then nodded, the resolve in his eyes matching my own. We knew it was the only way to protect our son.

The worker looked serious and obviously tired when she came back. After inhaling deeply, my ex started talking, his voice wavering. With every word, he described the events exactly as they had occurred, and we were able to let go of the fear that had seized us.

The worker listened, her face taking on a dark, angry look. When he was done, she got up quickly. "This should have been told to me from the beginning," she yelled. "You now have to arrange for a family member to take the children. After this lying, I can't let any of them stay with either of you."

Her remarks were a kick in the gut, but they also served as an alarming reminder of the results of what we did. Reality set in as we fear trying to get in touch with family members. We were now suffering the price for allowing others to direct us, and our fears to rule us.

Making contact with family created a storm of conflicting feelings. I wouldn't say that the majority of my immediate family and I had a tight, trustworthy relationship. Every call seemed like a desperate plea and an open confession of my weaknesses. I approached both sides of the family his and mine for assistance, as did my ex, but they insisted that someone from my side to take in all three of my children. They wanted to keep my kids together even though we were married, especially since my oldest child didn't belong to my ex-husband.

After much consideration from both of us, my older sister decided to take the lead. She was thrown into a role that she had not requested, accepting a duty that took away her calm and added to her already heavy load. She took action because she could not oversee the idea of my kids being placed with the state or in foster care.

Every time we spoke, I could see the tension in her eyes and hear it in her voice. She was trying her hardest to maintain order and give my kids some sense of normalcy in the middle of the destruction. However, it was evident that the circumstances were wearing her down. The unanticipated burden of taking care of three additional children was added to the responsibilities of her own life, and it was more than she could manage at the time.

I felt terrible because I knew that this load had been placed on her by my decisions and circumstances. I was deeply appreciative, but I also didn't know how much it would cost. My sister paid a heavy price for her wellbeing, yet her sacrifice kept my kids out of the system.

The social worker moved quickly to have my sister authorized to be my children's guardian parent. As we awaited the last word, every second seemed to take forever. At last, the worker reappeared bearing a pile of paperwork and a determined look.

With a forceful voice, she stated, "Your sister has been approved to take custody of your children." "These documents must be signed by both parents."

We exchanged a look of relief and resignation, me, and my ex. With shaky hands, we walked slowly to the table and signed each document. There was a strange, out-of-body feeling to it. The awful reality of our predicament was beginning to set in.

After signing the final document, the worker collected them up and gave us a harsh look. "You must immediately exit this room. Do not go visit or pick up your other two kids. It has been two days since you last saw them, and it will not happen until we appear in court. As soon as I have all the information, I will share it.

Her remarks struck me like a sledgehammer, making me feel deeply affected by the situation's finality and severity. We left the room together, my ex and I walking away in silence that was full of regrets and hidden concerns. It hurt so much to think that I would never be able to see or hold my kids. The long journey ahead and the reality of decisions had to be faced.

As I left the building, tears streamed down my face, each one a testament to the pain and uncertainty gnawing at my soul. My mind raced with questions that had no immediate answers. When would I see my kids again? Would they be loved and treated well, or would they face the same harsh treatment I had endured growing up? The memories of my own childhood, the way my sister had treated me when my mother was in prison, flooded back with a vengeance.

Together with the new pain of the present, the weight of my past transgressions weighed heavily on me. I was overcome with a sense of remorse and feeling defeated since I knew that our decisions had led us to this situation. It was nearly unbearable to think about my children going through the same suffering I had because I was afraid history would repeat itself.

In that moment, standing in the cold, brutal light of reality, I vowed to do everything in my power to right things. Though the road ahead would not be easy and would present many obstacles, I had to have faith that the broken things could be repaired. For myself, for my kids, and for the prospect of a brighter tomorrow.

Chapter 9
Kicking Me While I am Down

Her comments struck me in the heart, persistent and unrelenting, like sharp arrows piercing my mind. Every scathing remark and criticism echoed in my mind like an unrelenting drumbeat, a vicious symphony that preyed on my fears. What began as a temporary arrangement for my sister to watch my children while I weathered the storm turned into a living hell.

It appeared to be the answer to my prayers at first. Through our phone talks, I could hear my children laughing, their excitement providing a glimmer of optimism that this might actually work. I briefly thought we might be able to hang on, that perhaps this makeshift arrangement might help to stabilize the ground beneath us.

However, when the pressure of reality becomes too great, optimism has a nasty way of vanishing. At first, the peace broke down in tiny, nearly invisible ways. My baby's scream in the middle of the night. My sister's abrupt tone changes. The warmth she originally provided was gradually erased by the frustration that seeped into her remarks.

Every day her critiques grew more scathing. Not only were they words, but they were also judgments and weapons that ripped into the already brittle fragments of my self-worth. She spoke with direct words. Every irritation and difficulty I faced while raising my kids seemed to be my fault. Every choice I made and action I did was distorted by her contempt, which eventually caused me to start doubting the core of my identity as a mother.

Our tension escalated to an intolerable level. Our conversations were tense with implicit hostility, and we snapped over the simplest things. Her scrutiny was so intense that my shortcomings were painfully visible. Her remarks brought back memories of the setbacks I had experienced as a child, as if I were doomed to perpetuate the cycle of inadequacy that I had promised to avoid.

The world weighed heavily on me as I balanced long hours at the postal service. I was haunted by my ex's imprisonment; his inexcusable acts kept coming back to me like a nightmare I couldn't get out of. My lawyer demanded payment, I had a mountain of bills, and CPS wanted answers I didn't know how to explain. I felt too damaged to win the battle, and the pledge I made to defend my family was slipping away from me.

I know my sister wanted to contribute in her own way and meant well. However, her assistance was wrapped in barbed wire, which kept me confined to her house while she continued living her life. I felt like a prisoner in her place for hours on end, and every time I was separated from my children, my heart broke. Knowing that my children were all I could cling to in a world that seemed to be slipping away from me, I cherished all the time I did spend with them.

The breaking point occurred one day during a visit with my children. With an unwavering and hard stare, my sister stood before me and threatened that I would never again see my children—not until the courts ruled differently. What little willpower I still had was shattered by the words, which struck me like a hammer. With my desperation leaking into the air around us, I exploded, screaming and crying. It was grief, pure and genuine, not simply anger. It was the pain of being separated from my kids and of passively watching as someone else made decisions that affected my family's future.

I had already lost four months of my newborn's life. I hadn't kissed his little hands enough, rocked him to sleep enough, or held him long enough. Postpartum depression weighed heavy on my chest, depriving me of hope and breath. However, something in me hardened during that depressing moment.

The fight for custody was no longer the only issue. I fought for my soul, my identity as a mother, and the family I couldn't let go of. I couldn't be defined by my sister's words, opinions, or deeds. My resolve was just as real as the suffering.

Even though I was raw and shaking as I stood on that front lawn, there was something inside of me that was more intense than the terror. I was battling to regain my strength, my voice, and my position in my children's lives, not simply against my sister or the system. I refused to allow anyone else write the conclusion of my story since it wasn't finished yet.

Carelessly at first, like a wave slowly coming in, it swept me under. Her help initially felt like a lifeline, a brittle boat during a storm that I couldn't manage on my own. Her once-welcoming house quickly turned into a battlefield as her remarks got sharper and her tone colder. It felt like a hard punch to the chest the day she looked me in the eye and said, "You'll never see your kids again—at least not until the courts say so." I was out of breath from the anguish of her words, which went deeper than any bruise. I was an outsider, defenseless, and at her mercy in that instant; I wasn't a mother or a sister.

Underneath every encounter, her frustration boiled over into harsh comments that made me doubt my value as a mother. She once said, "Maybe they're better off without you," and her words cut like glass through me. I attempted to clarify and protest, but the force of her power overshadowed my voice. Every unhealed wound between us was compounded by the stress of our circumstances, which brought our challenging past into the present. She grabbed control of the one thing that mattered most to me—my children—and I felt like a child again, afraid to defend myself. It was as though all of my prior failures had returned with a vengeance, escalating our toxic relationship, and denying me a voice in a conflict I had no idea how to win.

I discovered that our doubts, whether they originate from ourselves or from others, do not define who we are. The decisions we make in response to those voices are what make us who we are. During my lowest points, I learned that no one else's opinions or deeds define my worth as a mother, sister, or woman. It stems from my steadfast love, my will to stand up for what is most important, and my reluctance to give up no matter how difficult the road ahead may appear.

Let my narrative serve as an inspiration of hope for everyone who has ever felt hopeless, broken, or overwhelmed by the weight of their situation. You possess the inner strength to take back your voice, change the narrative, and overcome the obstacles that are trying to keep you down. Your value is determined by your bravery in getting back up and moving on, not by the suffering you go through.

This taught me that even though life may knock us down, each setback presents a chance to get back up and try again. Take the first move, no matter how tiny, in the direction of healing, power restoration, and a better, more resilient future. Even if the darkness can persist, your light is more powerful. Allow it to shine.

Words were my lifeline during those times when I felt helpless and purposeless. I was able to release the hurt, rage, and powerlessness I was unable to convey throughout those struggles through poetry. Among the poems I composed at the time, this one is an honest depiction of my inner conflict:

I'm already down why are you kicking me?

I am a mess down in the depths where shadows play.
You stand there, hand in hand, kicking me where I lie even though I've already fallen.
But pay close attention and I'll tell you; your punches won't break my spirit.

Even if I fall and get hurt, I get back up stronger than before.
I will discover my light in the clutches of darkness, standing firm against the deepest night.
My determination to overcome fear and stand strong is becoming more evident with every hit.
Therefore, feel free to push me down, but know that my spirit will never tarnish.
Because no matter what happens, I will climb above the depths where shadows dance.

More than just a way to vent my emotions, this poem marked a major shift and served as a mirror reflecting both my extreme hurt and my resiliency. I started to find my voice again and realize how strong I was, even in the middle of my sorrow, after reading those sentences.

Chapter 10
Rage Igniting: A Mother's Resolve

The echoes of their laughing echoed through the now cold and dead rooms of the deserted house. Every portrait on the wall was a bitter echo of happier times, and every unplayed with toy was a mute reminder of their absence. A deep, unending longing for the warmth of my children's presence burned in my heart, a pain that only a mother could comprehend.

I struggled with the weight of my reality as I stood in isolation. In my quest to be reunited with my children, the system that was meant to protect and serve me had turned into an intimidating wall that seemed impassable. I couldn't stop wondering: Why hadn't I been summoned to court? Why did I continue to wait for an opportunity to prove myself? The injustice I experienced was oppressive, and the suspicions expressed by people I used to trust made it even more painful.

I didn't back down, though. Before any court order dictated my behavior, I sought knowledge and attended a parenting class at the Home of Innocence because I was determined to take charge of what I could. It was a positive move, a brief but impactful statement of my will to do whatever I needed to get my kids home.

I eventually appeared in court as the days stretched into weeks and weeks into months. My anxiety and resolve were further heightened by the sterile walls and cold looks. A caseworker was tasked by the court to keep an eye on me in my house with my children. Her visits, which were always around 8:30am, occurred right after I finished my nightly shifts at 6:00am, leaving me exhausted but determined.

It was depressing and infuriating news that the caseworker brought. Once my rock, my mother and sister had come out against me, casting doubt on my stability and characterizing me as an angry person. Their judgmental and treacherous words rang so loudly that I was left reeling. But in the middle of their lies, I noticed that my voice was becoming louder.

My mission became clear when my daughter courageously told the caseworker and I about the inhumane treatment she received from my sister— being made to eat food she threw away from a trash can. My sister admitted to doing so when questioned about it. I was more needed than ever by my kids. Although hearing her words caused me terrible agony, they ignited a fire inside of me. I made the decision to be their steadfast advocate, guided by the social work code of ethic tenets, which highlight the value and dignity of every person, especially children who are at risk which happen to be my own at this time.

I realized that no one could love my kids as much as I did. Every battle, every tear, and every restless night were worth it for their rights, their welfare, and their futures. Restoring the sense of security, love, and stability they were entitled to was more important than simply getting children home; I would do everything in my power to accomplish this goal.

In the midst of my turmoil, I contacted parents who had gone through similar experiences in the hopes that their insights might clarify my own ambiguous path. Every story I heard was a strand in a resilient quilt that told a story of hope in the face of adversity. While some talked about minor triumphs that gave them newfound strength to battle, others revealed heartbreaking experiences that made me feel overwhelmed by my own anxieties. These talks served as a lifeline and a mirror, reflecting my feelings of vulnerability as well as the strength I was starting to discover.

My determination was strengthened by the combination of sympathy and friendship I discovered in those early discussions. It served as a reminder that, despite the lonely anguish of being apart from my kids, I wasn't alone. I gained new resolve with each encouraging word—the conviction that I, too, could get past the challenges I faced.

Motivated by this renewed optimism, I made the decision to act. In an effort to demonstrate my preparedness to be reunited with my children, I signed up for a six-week parenting program. Love and an unshakeable will to do everything in my power to bring my children home drove my decision.

However, looking back, my eagerness to show myself was my downfall. I was still unaware of the complex web of red tape that lay ahead. Despite my good intentions, my decision to act exposed my ignorance of the legal system. Unaware that I didn't need the classes, and the fact my ex couldn't be in the home with me and the children would make things even more difficult, I had thought that taking initiative-taking steps would be enough to prove my capacity as a parent.

Nevertheless, each lesson I took served as evidence of my commitment. I learned how to be a better parent with every lesson, but I also came to understand that I was fighting for the stability and life we all deserved, not just for my kids.

It was two months before my court appearance which seemed to drag on forever. I pondered why I hadn't been given the chance to present my case yet, and every day was a struggle against powerlessness and frustration. The promise that I would see a judge within thirty days was broken, leaving me to drown for weeks of unresolved issues and growing doubt. Not only was time squandered, but the prolonged silence heightened my doubts and anxieties, leading me to wonder if the system genuinely wanted justice for my family.

The courtroom was just as massive as I had thought it would be on the day that eventually came. The rows of benches appeared to echo the weight of many other lives judged within those walls, while the space's formality was reflected in the stark walls and polished floors. As I waited for my case to be called, there was a noticeable sense of tension and an absent rush of excitement.

Every word I said in front of the judge had the weight of my future. Not only did the gavel strike wood, but it also struck my resolve. The system suddenly became apparent to me as a maze, an intimidating maze of regulations, verdicts, and choices that were beyond of my control. However, my resolve remained unwavering despite the overwhelming magnitude of the work at hand.

This was the first concrete step in my battle for my kids, and I promised to face this obstacle head-on with unyielding determination. Despite the fact that the courtroom was a battleground, I was prepared to fight for what was most important reuniting my family.

The caseworker's visits were equally emotionally taxing. I was terrified of not living up to my expectations, but I was determined to show the greatest version of myself. With my kids' futures on the line, every visit felt like a test. I told myself that these sacrifices were just temporary, despite the cost. Every restless night and every last bit of effort was an investment in reuniting my family.

The betrayal hit me like a ton of bricks. I was portrayed as unstable and inept by my mother and sister, the exact people I had believed would support me through this process. My own blood became a weapon against me as their words went deeper than any blade. Their charges tainted the courts view of my life as they confidently discussed my alleged inadequacies.

Their admiration of my ex-partner, in addition to their criticism, was what hurt me the most. They disregarded the hardships I had faced in silence, the evenings spent dealing with the consequences of his drinking and the toll it took on our family. Their purposeful and agonizing omission made him appear trustworthy, while I was left to bear the entire blame.

I felt alone as a result of the distortion of my reality, as though I were battling not just the system but also the individuals who ought to have supported me. I decided to shine brighter despite their depiction of the truth, which was a shadow obscuring my light. I couldn't let their remarks define who I was or lessen my devotion to and affection for my kids.

I discovered a new type of power in that loneliness—a resolve to take back my voice and share my story in a way that would not be disregarded or altered. Although their betrayal was painful, it strengthened my determination to show that I was more than the person they had chosen to portray.

The love that never gives up is your strength, parents. Keep this in mind while you stand in the fire. Hold fast to your aim even when it seems impossible, when the system seems to be against you, and when you are feeling doubtful yourself. Your determination is your armor, and your love is your weapon. Your children are depending on you to speak up for them when their voices are not heard, so take a brave stand.

You will be evaluated by adversity, but it won't define you. Every obstacle I encountered presented a chance to conquer it and demonstrate that love, tenacity, and hope are stronger than even the most hopeless circumstances. Keep in mind that a parent's resolve, driven by an unshakable link, has the capacity to transform everything. Take a proud stance. Fight hard. And never, ever forget that you are your children's source of hope, their pillar of support, and their inspiration that no fight is too big for them to overcome. Every tear, every sacrifice, and every victory are worth it for them. You are stronger than you realize, so keep going.

The judge's words, "The children are to be returned to their mother immediately," broke through the doubt, fear, and uncertainty that had dominated my life for so long as the gavel came down. My heart swelled with a delight I hadn't had in months, and time stopped as tears clouded my vision. It was done. I was victorious. I had fought for my children—and I had won—against every challenge, every falsehood, and every doubt that had been thrown at me.

The once cold and lifeless house seemed to come alive again when I and my children entered the door for the first time I months. The rooms were filled with love and warmth as their laughing bounced off the walls. Every embrace, kiss, and hushed "I love you" was a promise to them and to myself that nothing would ever keep us apart now that we are together again.

I had a great feeling of purpose and thankfulness that night as I nestled them into the bed with me and watched their peaceful faces fall asleep. "You will always be safe with me," I said, kissing their foreheads and leaving a lasting impression. Nothing, not even a lie or a miscommunication, will ever be able to take you away from me again. I promised them then and there that I would always love, care for, and treasure them with the passionate loyalty that only a mother could provide.

Know that you are stronger than the storm you are facing if you are still fighting your war. It's worth every tear you cry, every restless night, and every last bit of your hard work. It is impossible to extinguish the light of your love for your children. It will assist you rise over the tallest fences and lead you through the deepest valleys of water.

It is possible to win. Remain true to yourself, put your all into defending your family, and never give up. Because love always wins in the end.

Chapter 11
Suicide Cannot Have My Life

Have you ever had the sensation that everything was pressing down on you so hard that it was difficult for you to breathe? Have you ever been at a place when it looked like there was no more hope for your future, and you were left feeling hopeless and like you had nothing left to live for? It's difficult to see a path ahead when belief seems distant and feeling defeated seems imminent. Even still, the tiniest glimmer of resilience can frequently start a path towards recovery and rejuvenation when such intense feelings are at their lowest.

Yes, that was me. It all began to happen again when I lost everything for which I had sacrificed a great deal. It seemed as though the earth had been torn from under my feet one moment, and the next I was standing tall, secure in the life I had created. I was surrounded by a depressing veil of hopelessness and a terrible sense of loss. I was haunted by the recollections of my past self and felt hollow, like a shadow of my old self. There seemed to be an unquenchable emptiness left behind by the dreams and goals I had fostered and chased with unwavering determination. Sadness was an unwelcome guest that would not go; it was a heavy, persistent presence. It was a daily struggle against the overpowering tide of hopelessness, and I began to wonder if it was worth it to keep going at all.

My sense of direction had vanished along with my relationship with God. It was as if my GPS had completely stopped functioning, leaving me lost and unable to find my way in the middle of nowhere. During my lowest points, I had the impression that I was stranded on the side of the road by myself, abandoned by millions of cars whose taillights vanished into the horizon. Every passing car served as an unpleasant confirmation of the life that was going on all around me, while I stayed motionless, hopeless, and confused. All I saw in front of me was the wide, empty road, yet I kept looking for a sign, some indication of God's purpose. I was left to work through the uncertainties and try to figure out why my life had taken such a detour on my own. I was incredibly alone, and I hurt a lot. I started doubting everything I had ever believed in, trying to find purpose in the isolation.

It all began after I was placed in front of the Professional Standards Unit (PSU) in a sterile room after a second investigation was launched against me. There was a knot of worry in my stomach when they started questioning me. I can still picture a chill running down my back as I fought not to give in to the fear that everyone would be listening to everything I said. I couldn't bring myself to be honest in spite of my dread. I became suspicious and began telling lies because I thought the system was biased against me. I thought they were more concerned with defending themselves than they were with learning the truth. With the knowledge I have, the department's foundation might be torn apart, revealing systemic corruption. I had always believed in ethics and doing the right thing, even before any of these investigations got underway. It appeared that these exact values would now be the department's undoing, and I found myself caught in the crossfire, trying to make my way through an extremely dangerous circumstance where trust was an expense I couldn't afford.

After leaving PSU, I returned home with a whirlwind of ideas and feelings. The scale of what had happened was intolerable. I confronted the truth of my anxieties, understanding that the lies I'd told—the words I thought would soothe my pain—had actually entangled me further in a case of confusion. I had told them what they wanted to hear in the hopes that it would shorten my suffering, but it simply heightened my anguish. The truth about my perpetrator, which had been suppressed from me, felt like a betrayal, as if the same institution supposed to protect me had failed.

I knew then how hopeless I was, that depression had already crept into my life and shadowed everything I had once loved, but I had made a decision, I had decided to show up and coach my little league basketball team, and I knew that the young faces watching me relied on me, even though my heart weighed heavily, and I walked onto that court, coaching with a hollow enthusiasm, my spirit barely fluttering under the weight of my tears.

As the game progressed, I was torn between those children's happiness and my own sorrow, their laughing echoing in my ears like a far-off piece of hope. However, as soon as the last whistle blew, I withdrew once more into the privacy of my dimly lit chamber, where the comforting embrace of loneliness wrapped me like a blanket.

Nevertheless, I felt a glimmer of fortitude—a tiny, rebellious spark that pushed me to stand even amid that gloom. Every cry I shed felt liberating, like a stride back toward my truth. I realized that even if the road ahead was unclear, it was up to me to find my way. I started to see that, despite its difficulties, my journey could become a story of perseverance and fortitude. I was committed to escaping the shadows, transforming my suffering into meaning, and emerging not only as a survivor but also as a beacon of hope for anyone who might be feeling hopeless in their own darkness.

The typical process of getting ready for work felt like an uphill battle, so I headed to the bathroom knowing I needed to find strength. I switched on the water and let it run while I collected my thoughts. I yelled, "Alexa, play Tamela Mann radio," thinking the tune would take my mind off of my misery. Kirk Franklin's "My World Needs You" was the first music to fill the air, and I immediately fell to my knees, finding comfort in prayer but it wasn't working.

The idea of escape, of permanently silencing my pain, slipped into my consciousness, luring me with the illusion of peace, and I imagined a life where my problems simply faded away, where I wouldn't be a burden to anyone. As the melody wrapped me, my mind started to spiral, and I found myself thinking about what the world would be like without me—a haunting thought that wrapped me in a fetal position, my heart heavy with the weight of dissatisfaction

But in the depths of that darkness, I felt a numbness wash over me, a disconnect from the very essence of life. I lost sight of my children's laughter, my mother's love, and the bond I shared with my siblings. The thought of leaving them behind, of shattering their lives in my wake, was a fleeting whisper against the cacophony of my pain.

In that vulnerable moment, as the water cascaded around me, I began to realize that this wasn't just about me. It was about the lives intertwined with mine—the love that would be left behind, the questions that would linger, the hearts that would ache. I was not alone in this fight, even if it felt that way. The music played on, carrying a message I desperately needed to hear: my world needed me.

Slowly, the realization began to pierce through the fog. I could choose to fight. I could reach out for help, for understanding, for the strength to carry on. This was a pivotal moment, a turning point where I could either succumb to the darkness or rise up and face it head-on. With each passing note, I felt the stirrings of hope begin to awaken within me, a flicker igniting the possibility of a new chapter, one where I could transform my pain into a source of strength, not just for myself, but for those who loved me.

I walked into work, my heart still heavy, and realized I was over an hour late. As I settled into my new job on the line, tears slipped down my cheeks, no matter how hard I tried to fight them back. Just then, my supervisor called me into her office.

"Is everything okay?" she asked, concern etched across her face.

I took a deep breath, feeling the floodgates open. "I'm not okay," I admitted, my voice trembling. "I feel like I have absolutely nothing to live for." I broke down, the weight of my despair crashing over me.

She looked at me with empathy in her eyes. "Do you believe in God? Do you pray?"

"Yes, ma'am," I replied, still sobbing.

"Can I pray for you?" she asked gently. I nodded yes, and as she prayed, I felt a glimmer of something—a tiny thread of hope weaving through my pain. Then she shared a story that struck me deep.

"My brother took his life," she said, her voice shaking. "The pain of not being able to see or talk to him anymore is something I carry with me every day. I wish I could have done more to help him."

Her words hung in the air, and for the first time, I felt understood.

"Would you consider going to therapy?" she asked, her gaze steady.

I hesitated. "People are going to think I'm crazy for real."

"No, they won't," she reassured me. "You'll be strong for taking that step. You have so much more in store for you—you're beautiful, determined, and intelligent. Don't forget that."

That conversation ignited a spark within me. I decided to take the leap into therapy, even though it meant accepting short-term disability and living on 60% of my pay. Anxiety twisted in my gut at the thought of my bills piling, but she said something that stayed with me: "Don't worry about your bills; focus on your faith and trust in God."

In that moment, I felt a shift. Maybe I did not have to carry this weight alone. Maybe, just maybe, there was a path forward—a chance to reclaim my life, one small step at a time.

This taught me that one day, the hardships that seem impossible now might serve as the testimony that saves another life. Every tear shed and ounce of strength mustered is not in vain; rather, it is strengthening resilience and paving the way for a better future.

Being honest with yourself, seeking therapy, and having religion can all be lifesavers rather than flaws. It takes courage to choose to heal, and even a little beginning step might result in a transformation you never would have imagined.

This phase of my life serves as a reminder to me that I have never traveled a difficult path alone. I extended my hand, waited, and had faith that the same force that got me through yesterday would strengthen me for today. Keep in mind that the world needs you—your love, your light, your unique purpose. Your best days are still to come, and you are here for a reason.

Chapter 12

Change My Life

On January 1, 2021, which was also my 33rd birthday, when the clock struck midnight, I was thinking back on the path that had led me to this point in a luxurious hotel room in Houston, Texas. I chose to begin this momentous day with prayer, inspired by Psalm 61:2, "From the ends of the earth I call to you, I call as my heart grows faint; lead me to the rock that is higher than I," while I was surrounded by the comforts of my improvised sanctuary. I set out on a profound journey of self-discovery and spiritual rejuvenation with these words as my guidance. Equipped with thirty-three affirmations every day, all of which are a gleam of sunshine and self-love, I made a commitment to take better care of myself and accept the fact that I am nothing without God. It was a turning point that determined my direction for the coming year, as I started on the journey of self-love and faith-based self-empowerment.

My mind raced with thoughts of the next day when I went to sleep that evening. When I woke up and saw the first rays of morning light coming through the curtains, I got ready for the day's activities. After grabbing a Lyft to take me to get a rental car, I got into the backseat and heard Dr. Eric Thomas's strong voice coming over the speakers. His comments, "You Can't Defeat Me," resonated deeply and established the tone for the day. Curious, I asked the Lyft driver, "Who's that playing on your radio?" turning to face him. He smiled sardonically and said, "Oh, that's 'ET'—he's a beast." I could feel my enthusiasm rising as I said, "I have to meet him. Actually, I'm going to get to know him." As we started making our way, the renewable power of what was ahead rushed through the vehicle we were in.

  I was inspired by Dr. Eric Thomas's motivational lectures and learned about him online. I was anxious to seek out his advice to help me get through times of uncertainty and doubt. I can clearly remember the rush of enthusiasm that greeted my choice to study his teachings more thoroughly in the hopes of finding inspiration and support to keep on and fulfill my mission. But even though I was excited at first, when I realized I could attend his 120 virtual conference, panic set in. When it came to the idea of moving outside of my comfort zone, I wavered and eventually allowed fear to prevent me from taking advantage of the chance.

A few days later, I received a phone call from a woman by coincidence. It was like an instant reminder from the universe about the possibilities that awaited me if I decided to choose faith over fear. This unexpected turn of events gave me encouragement, and I decided to stop isolating myself and start a journey of empowerment and self-discovery. Seeing how my experiences affected other women, I found comfort and meaning in telling my story and fearlessly faced the obstacles I overcame with the resolute help of my religion. After giving my experience some thought, I realized that it was more than just a personal battle; rather, it was a testimony to the human spirit's tenacity and the ability of faith to transform even in the face of adversity.

Woman on the phone: Hi there, is this Ebony Johnson?

Me: Yes, speaking. Who's this?

Woman on the phone: Hi, I'm with Eric Thomas and Associate. I noticed you started filling out the application for the

120 virtual conferences. We wanted to reach out and see if you were still interested in attending.

Me: I got scared and hung up.

Woman on the phone: Hey is this, Ebony?

Me: Yes, how may I help you?

Woman on the phone: Why did you hang up? Are you still interested in attending the conference?

Me: Oh, hi! Yes, I was interested, but I got a bit scared and stopped halfway through the application.

Woman on the phone: That's completely understandable. These opportunities can be intimidating at first. But I'm glad you picked up the phone. We're really excited about this event, and we think you'd benefit greatly from it.

Me: I'm sure I would, but honestly, I can't afford it right now.

Woman on the phone: No worries at all. We actually have a sponsorship program. Would you be interested in being a sponsor?

Me: Um, I hadn't thought about that. But sure, if it helps me attend, why not?

Woman on the phone: Fantastic! Thank you so much for your willingness to support. Could you provide us with a vertical and horizontal flyer featuring your logo and a message that aligns with it?

Me: Absolutely, I can get that sorted for you right away. Just give me a moment.

[After sending the flyer]

Woman on the phone: Perfect! This looks great. Thank you for your promptness. We'll get everything sorted for your sponsorship.

Me: Thank you. I'm really looking forward to attending the conference and being a part of this opportunity.

I was filled with excitement when I signed into the virtual 120 conference. The quiet of my tiny, painstakingly organized workstation was broken by the gentle sound of my laptop. I had a notebook open to a new page, a pen ready to write every word, and a steaming cup of Starbucks herbal tea on my desk. In the middle of the excitement, I was grounded by the gentle scent of peaches and peppermint that dominated the air.

I rearranged my chair so that I was facing the camera, and my background was a reflection of who I am: a plain wall with inspirational sayings and a framed certificate from my organization, Encouraging Minds. Knowing that this was the start of a new era, I wanted to demonstrate professionalism and genuineness.

My heart was pounding as the screen's countdown clock approached the first session. With a splash of upbeat music and a modern, animated logo, the conference officially started as the screen flickered. At that point, the moderator's voice could be heard: "Greetings from the 120 Virtual Conference! All of you, including our incredible sponsors, are very welcome. An extra shoutout goes out to Encouraging Minds, whose goal is to teach individuals that it's acceptable to not feel okay and to not ignore their emotions.

I felt both proud and shocked when I heard my nonprofit's name called out. I hurriedly pushed away the tears that welled up in my eyes, reminding myself to maintain my composure. I held my pen firmly as the session progressed, excitement building within of me.

The opening video montage, which included excerpts of ET in action, success stories, and clips from previous conferences, was a masterclass in inspiration. Even through the computer screen, you could feel the intensity. I experienced a thrilling mixture of anxiety and excitement, prepared to absorb all of the knowledge that lay ahead of me.

The mood in my room seemed to change as ET arrived on the screen. His presence, even on a virtual stage, was imposing. He leaned into the camera, his piercing eyes meeting the virtual audience's, his words ringing with conviction, all while wearing a simple yet confident outfit. He said, "What's up, family?!" in a tone that was both kind and forceful. "You want to transform your life, which is why you're here. Let me tell you something, though:

simply because you showed up, change won't happen. You must appear!" Something within me was sparked by his words, which struck like sparks. Every syllable had fire and rhythm, drawing me in and requiring all of my focus.

His voice rose and fell with the rhythm of a pulpit preacher as he recounted his path of hardship, determination, and faith. He once stopped, stared straight into the camera, and said, "You have to do something you haven't done before if you want something you haven't had before. In order to progress, are you willing to endure discomfort? I was startled by the inquiry, which made me feel a sense of urgency. "You have excellence within you," he said without apology. However, it will remain incarcerated unless you talk to it, feed it, and care for it. Use the key you have!" His comments felt like they were written specifically for my path, and his passion was genuine and relevant. By the time his introduction was over, I wasn't only observing; I was actively participating, prepared to take on the task and live the life I was destined to lead. In my spirit, ET had stoked a flame that would not go out.

In unexpected ways, the conference forced me to face my anxieties and embrace my vulnerabilities. I was initially hesitant to participate in breakout conversations because I was worried that my ideas might not be sufficient. However, as the sessions went on, I discovered that I was embracing the discomfort, being honest about my experiences, and paying close attention to what others had to say. It was both enlightening and humble to get constructive criticism because it made me aware of my blind spots, which I had been too scared to address. I was able to shed my ego and embrace a growth attitude by using each piece of advice as a steppingstone. I started to realize that being coachable meant being open to learning and growing rather than having all the answers.

Connecting with another participant whose narrative reflected aspects of mine was one of the most life-changing experiences I had. Their tenacity and viewpoint caused me to reevaluate my journey and generated concepts I had not before thought of. This connection made me realize how important it is to invest in relationships, not only as a networking tactic but also as a means of encouraging support and progress for both parties. By the time the conference ended, I had developed valuable relationships that strengthened the idea of group empowerment in addition to acquiring the skills I needed to change both my personal and professional life.

Chapter 13
Breaking Free from Shame and Fear

For a large portion of my life, shame and fear shaped my choices and interactions like unwelcome guests who were always there but silent. They wove themselves into my identity and whispered doubts in my ears when I wanted to feel confident. These feelings flourished under the shadow of poverty and uncertainty, growing up in a household where surviving was a daily struggle. Their weight created a lens of inadequacy that influenced not just how I saw myself but also how I believed others saw me. But over those hazy years, a glimmer of fortitude remained, a silent but steadfast reminder that I was more than my situation. This chapter describes how, in my journey as a social worker, I discovered that the emerald, stoked its flames, and discovered how to free myself from the bond.

Growing up in poverty was more than simply a situation; it was a way of life that affected every aspect of my life. Rather than feeling like a haven, our house felt more like a patchwork of survival. Stories of unpaid bills were related in the dimly lit rooms, and the peeling paint appeared to reflect the gradual deterioration of hopes that poverty frequently brings. The shattered and taped-up blinds on the windows provided a warped vision of a world that seemed so far away. There was a weight even in the air in our home, a subliminal awareness that we were on the edge, balancing on the brink of losing everything and barely surviving.

The criticism at school was more nuanced but just as harsh. I bore the unseen weight of "less than" in classrooms full of kids who seemed so carefree. Too tight or too loose, my hand-me-downs felt like a billboard proclaiming my uniqueness. Even though I couldn't always hear what my classmates were saying, I could sense their meaning when they whispered or giggled and looked at me. The cafeteria was a battleground in and of itself; I would sit and enjoy the free lunch the school provided while pretending not to notice when others unwrapped carefully packed homemade lunches. An unwritten rule that I didn't belong appeared to be reinforced by every encounter.

The fight intensified within. I longed to blend in, to laugh with my friends without feeling alienated, but every effort felt forced, as if my very existence validated my deception. Poverty was more than simply a lack of money; it was a constant reminder that I was "different." The strain of these unspoken criticisms caused my self-esteem to deteriorate. My own thoughts persuaded me that I wasn't enough the more I tried to fit in.

At home, the silence was deafening. We didn't talk about the hard things—not the empty refrigerator, not the eviction notices, not the nights spent under blankets because the heat and lights had been shut off again. Fears were swallowed, buried deep inside, because speaking to them aloud felt dangerous, as though acknowledging them might give them more power. Instead, the family's focus was survival, and emotions became luxuries we couldn't afford.

The teachings of poverty were discovered by necessity and observation rather than verbally. Nobody specifically instructed me to "don't talk about what you don't have," but I picked up the idea from the way my family avoided answering queries from neighbors or how we would sidestep discussions about birthdays or holidays that we couldn't observe. I learnt to keep quiet to protect myself, hoping that no one would see the holes in my facade.

The stigma of poverty got woven into my identity. One specific incident on a field trip in elementary school will always stick in my memory. A classmate produced a vibrantly colored lunchbox adorned with cartoon characters around lunchtime. It contained carefully packaged snacks and a message from their mother that said, "Enjoy your day! I love you. While I sat staring at my school lunch bag and gripping my stomach to keep it from growling, I strongly hoped that the earth would swallow me. It felt like a public statement of our struggle when I got my school "lunch," a mismatched bag full of wet bread and whatever the school had to provide. I could see the wonder in my friends' looks and the sympathy in my teacher's eyes.

However, it was about more than just food and material belongings; it was about what those things stood for. Everything that I lacked seemed to be another way for the outside world to validate my fears that I was flawed and unworthy. I took these experiences to heart and applied them to every encounter. Together, the social criticisms at school and the emotional silence at home formed an invisible cage that influenced my perception of myself and how I believed the outside world regarded me.

Even as a young child, I saw that poverty was more than just a financial situation; it was a vicious circle of exclusion, humiliation, and quiet that deprived you of tangible belongings as well as the conviction that you were deserving of more. Years would pass before the seeds of self-doubt could be pulled up and replaced with something more resilient. However, I had no idea how to escape at that time. I was only aware of the weight of the unseen restraints.

The guilt and dread I had as a youngster followed me into adulthood, changing to suit my changing situation rather than magically disappearing. I can still clearly recall my 2006 high school graduation. Instead of being a time of pride, it was a moment of uncertainty. Uncertainty murmured in my ear as I got ready to enroll at Benedict College that August as a social work major, wondering if I really fit. Then I discovered I was expecting a child. When I compared myself to my friends, who exuded confidence and walked with a confidence I couldn't even pretend, my self-doubt was at its loudest. Their journeys seemed seamless, but mine was paved with unseen barriers: the burden of my background, the worry that my difficulties diminished my potential, and the persistent doubt about my ability to achieve in life. Since there were others who had experienced identical circumstances to mine, I had absolutely no reason for comparing myself to others.

Those emotions of inadequacy persisted when I enrolled at the University of Louisville in January of 2021 to gain my Bachelor of Social Work (BSW). I felt like I was walking a tightrope because of my personal issues, between the demands of a career that emphasizes empowerment with my own internalized notion that who I am is defined by my history. I was afraid that people would view me as unsuited for this job if they knew about my past—poverty, shame, and the crippling self-doubt that occasionally affected me. My perception of my abilities was distorted by the false belief that adversity was a sign of weakness rather than resiliency.

In my social work classes, every task seemed more like a chance for failure than for improvement. I would question if I had the appropriate words, the appropriate viewpoint, or even the right to be in the room. Shame was more than simply a feeling; it was a lens through which I viewed the world and myself. I was persuaded that my wounds diminished my ability to succeed and, ironically, my capacity to aid in the healing of others.

My perspective on my narrative didn't change until I started my social work training. An instructor told a story about their own childhood hardships during a class. Their statements vividly demonstrated resilience—the ability to transform hardships into opportunities and suffering into meaning. It was similar to noticing a glimmer in a wall I had assumed was unbreakable. I became aware for the first time that I wasn't the only one who had these anxieties.

My own problems were reflected in the class talks from mentors and students. They talked about struggles I could identify with, such feeling like imposters in work situations, growing up in unstable environments, and wondering if their pasts prevented them from creating the future they want. I had never felt such a sense of bonding before because of these common experiences. What I had previously considered an unpleasant isolation turned into a means of cultivating relationships.

My realization that vulnerability was a strength rather than a weakness marked a major shift in my perspective. I realized that my past didn't have to limit me; in fact, it might serve as the basis for the work I wanted to pursue after learning how others had overcome comparable cycles of fear and guilt. Every story I heard during fieldwork—whether from a client, a professor, or a peer—served as a reminder that being resilient wasn't about acting as though the difficulties never occurred. The goal was to confront them directly and gain authority in the process.

That insight changed the way I saw things. My enthusiasm for social work was woven together by my hardships, which I didn't want to conceal. They provided me with depth, empathy, and the capacity to relate to people on a human level. I realized that my journey—every setback, uncertainty, and victory—was a testimonial to my ability to overcome rather than a sign of weakness.

The concept of treatment initially seemed like removing a bandage from a wound that would never completely heal. I did everything in my power to reject it. It was terrible to consider sitting across from someone, or perhaps a crowd, and exposing the guilt I had been carrying for so long. What if it validated my deepest worries that I was flawed, undeserving, and irreparable? Even when I set up my first therapy session in 2020, I spent the days before, persuading myself that I could manage things without it.

However, something started to change during those treatment sessions. The therapist's inquiries were straightforward but compassionate, revealing levels of self-criticism I was unaware existed. I initially suppressed my tears because I felt ashamed of my own weakness. Even I was accustomed to concealing my armor's flaws from myself. But gradually, the focus of the sessions shifted from avoiding pain to comprehending it.

One crucial point was raised during a conversation about resilience. "Why do you think you've made it this far?" my therapist questioned. I automatically redirected, attributing it to good fortune or outside assistance. However, they gently pressed, highlighting the decisions I had made, and the perseverance required to continue when the odds were stacked against me. For the first time, I considered myself to be resilient rather than only a situational survival.

The voice in my head that used to chastise me for every perceived failure gradually softened and was replaced by a stronger but quieter voice that affirmed my value. While therapy didn't make the difficulties go away, it did provide me with new perspectives on them. It reframed my difficulties as the soil from which my power had developed rather than as proof of my lack.

Going back to school to pursue social work was a lifeline, not just an intellectual endeavor. I developed a fresh perspective on my own challenges while I studied subjects like systemic injustices and trauma-informed care. What I used to think were isolated failures were actually a part of larger patterns that were influenced by uncontrollable factors. It was both devastating and empowering to learn about the ways that trauma, poverty, and neglect impact people and communities.

I made the connection between my past and future for the first time. Education evolved into a bridge from victimization to empowerment, not just a means of obtaining a degree. Every lesson and every task seemed to fit together like a puzzle. I came to see that I had a distinct perspective and empathy because of my life experiences, which were not something that could be taught in a textbook but were crucial in the social work area.

Understanding the idea of post-traumatic growth was one of the most interesting lessons. To me, the concept that suffering could serve as a driving force for constructive transformation was new. My story changed from one of "I've been through too much" to one of "I've learned so much." I now have the confidence to actively strive toward a better future for both myself, my kids, and other people, rather than just dreaming about it.

It wasn't just me who managed to escape the clutches of fear and guilt. Some people along the way recognized my potential while I was unable to. Mentors who provided direction, friends who listened without passing judgment, and coworkers who had faith in my capacity to change things.

I can still clearly recall one mentor in particular—a professor who took the time to get to know me and found the good in me where I saw only the bad. "Your superpower is your lived experience," she informed me. You will become an exceptional social worker because of it. Those remarks stuck with me because they contradicted the story I had been telling for a long time.

Her faith in me was transforming, not merely consoling. It made me realize how powerful seeing and being seen can be. Through my work as a social worker or just as a friend, mentor, or colleague, I came to see that the assistance I had received was a gift I could offer to others.

I now see how crucial it is to create environments where people are valued and understood. Creating such kinds of support networks for myself and other people has become a top focus for me. I'm dedicated to being the kind of person who reminds individuals they are more than their circumstances, whether that means supporting a client or providing support to a colleague who is having difficulties.

Learning, healing, and connecting have all been part of the process of breaking free. Although it hasn't been simple, each step has helped me get closer to realizing my life's ambition of becoming someone who loves their unique narrative and uses it to encourage and uplift others.

Always, fear had seemed like a wall, something to be avoided at all costs. I eventually came to view it differently, though, as something that might indicate progress rather than failure. When I had to present a project to my peers in a college classroom, it was one of the first times this change became evident. My hands were shaking, my heart was thumping, and my mind was racing with failure-related ideas. But I felt compelled to move onward. I stammered as I spoke, but suddenly the words came easily. By the conclusion, a weird, thrilling pride had taken the place of the fear that had paralyzed me. Despite facing it, I was able to overcome it.

It was much more intimidating to tell my experience for the first time. I wondered why anyone would want to hear about the embarrassment I carried. However, I was speaking for everyone who has ever felt invisible, unheard, or undeserving when I took the stage in front of that room. Applause broke the stillness as soon as I was done, and several even came forward to congratulated me for being so honest. I came to the realization that fear was a gateway that I needed to pass through in order to discover my voice, not a destination.

Putting money into myself was another courageous move. I went to storytelling and public speaking masterminds because I knew I needed to improve, not because I felt I was ready. Every time I stepped in front of a crowd, doubts and fear were present. However, I leaned into it rather than squirming away from it, using it as motivation to keep going.

I've discovered that fear is a partner on the journey to transformation rather than an indication of failure. It identifies the places that are ready for expansion. The goal of the lesson was to reframe my life as a sign that I was entering a realm beyond myself, rather than to eradicate it.

I used to think that resilience was only the ability to endure adversity. I believed it meant clenching my jaw, enduring discomfort, and coming out on the other side. However, as I've matured, I've come to understand that resilience is about thriving despite the difficulties and finding strength in the fight, not just about surviving.

A major factor in this change has been a deliberate reflection. As I reflected on my journey, I started to recognize trends that I had previously missed. Even though I wasn't aware of it at the time, I had learned something from every difficult event. Going without taught me how to be resourceful. My experiences of feeling invisible helped me develop empathy for those who have similar feelings. My experiences of falling taught me how to get back up.

Being resilient is not a passive process; it is an engaged one. It's about transforming the raw ingredients of suffering into something valuable. Finding ways to not just survive but also to develop, flourish, and build a life that embodies the fortitude forged in the furnace of hardship is what it is all about.

To me, flourishing requires inspiring others with my narrative. It means acknowledging that my past has equipped me rather than defined me. I have become more understanding, compassionate, and connected as a result of every encounter, no matter how unpleasant. And sharing it has given me a stronger sense of purpose.

Today, resilience means more than just getting by each day. It's about creating a future that celebrates my journey, one in which I see myself as a testimony to my triumphs rather than a byproduct of my past.

My personal experience with fear and guilt has greatly influenced my approach to social work. I now view each individual as a person with a story to tell, one that is frequently loaded with unseen scars and silent struggles, rather than as a case file. Because I understand what it's like to be criticized, I always try to greet people with an open mind when I sit across from them.

Many of the kids I have previously worked with remind me of myself when I was younger. They bear the same burden of shame and insecurity as I did. I was more than simply a social worker to them; I am a sympathetic person. I reassure them that their difficulties do not define them and that their value is independent of their possessions or experiences. Through one-on-one conversations and workshops, I would teach them about the value of self-love. I urged them to accept their stories as evidence of their strength rather than as causes for embarrassment.

Working with a young woman who suffered from low self-esteem as a result of ongoing bullying at school stands out as one very memorable experience. She shrugged off praises as though they couldn't possibly be true and avoided making eye contact. I demonstrated to her that her voice was important week after week. We collaborated on personal projects that allowed her to use art to express her experiences. I noticed a flicker of satisfaction in her eyes when she eventually showed her work to her classmates in the cottage—a minor but significant triumph in ending the pattern of self-doubt.

In social work, I aim to eliminate the underlying stigma that prevents individuals from prospering rather than merely addressing superficial problems. By encouraging resilience, I assist individuals and communities in realizing that adversity need not be a permanent punishment but rather an entrance to something better.

Authenticity is one of the most potent instruments I have found in my work. I was hesitant to talk about my personal issues early in my profession with instructors and classmates. I was afraid that giving too much away might come out as weak or unprofessional. However, I soon discovered that careful sharing of vulnerability can serve as a bridge.

Because they think no one else can relate to their suffering, individuals frequently feel alone in their suffering. Sharing elements of my narrative, such as the times I felt worthless or questioned my abilities, is not meant to be about me but rather to let them know they're not alone. It means I've been there, and I recognize you.

I once provided coaching to a young mother who was experiencing homelessness. She felt overburdened, embarrassed, and certain that she was failing her kids. In a particularly challenging session, I talked about my personal experiences of feeling "good enough." When she understood that I was there to walk with her rather than pass judgment, her shoulders grew softer. We were able to collaborate on a strategy to restore her self-esteem and provide stability for her family because of that moment of connection.

Knowing when to share your narrative to promote hope is what it means to be real, not sharing too much. It's about demonstrating to individuals that being vulnerable is a sign of connection and healing rather than a sign of weakness. By doing this, I've discovered that the trust we establish serves as the cornerstone for significant change.

I have discovered in social work that advocacy is about human connection, not just policy or programs. I'm not only helping others when I meet them where they are, share my truth, and support them in embracing theirs; I'm also continuing to overcome my own past. By working together, we can break down the obstacles preventing us from moving forward and create a resilient, strong, and hopeful future.

Know that your narrative does not finish here if you are caught in the clutches of fear and shame. It takes tremendous strength to face these feelings; it is not a sign of weakness. Shame flourishes in silence, but its power is taken away when you have the courage to confront and acknowledge it.

Perfection is not the goal of growth. It's not a straight line where you wake up one day confident and fearless. Growth is a complicated process that involves both failures and breakthroughs. It involves appreciating the little things, like standing up for yourself or letting go of the urge to be flawless and learning to be gentle with yourself when the old doubts come back.

Face the humiliation that tells you you're not good enough. Go one step closer to the life you deserve, no matter how tiny. Every effort count, whether it's going to therapy, telling your story, or just being kind to yourself when you're having a rough day. Your path is worthwhile, and you are not alone.

Breaking free from guilt and fear has altered not only how I perceive myself, but also how I approach the most critical roles in my life. As a parent, I've made a commitment to disrupting generational cycles by educating my kids that their value comes from who they are rather than what they accomplish. I've learned to be there for them as an honest, caring, and present parent—not as a flawless one.

I no longer feel the need to appear to be in control of relationships. Deeper relationships, whether with friends, family, or coworkers, now start with vulnerability. And as an aspiring social worker, I view my background as a bridge that enables me to connect with people in a genuine and life-changing way rather than as an unnecessary expense.

It is my hope that readers will view their challenges as chances for personal development rather than obstacles. Every obstacle you overcome is making you a more resilient, sophisticated, and sympathetic person. The ability to rise above adversity, rather than the lack of it, is what makes you unique.

The process of overcoming fear and shame is a continuous one rather than a single victory. Even though there will be days when you feel like the past is dragging you back, the progress you've made will still be visible. Slow transformation occurs when you choose compassion over criticism, connection over isolation, and bravery over fear.

My experience serves as evidence that you can overcome extreme self-doubt and take back your life. I have the chance to witness this reality in the lives of people who have the courage to face their challenges and accept their resiliency since I'll be working as a social worker. I'll let this chapter serve as a reminder that you are more than your mistakes, your anxieties, and your past.

The daring to hope, the strength to grow, and the love you choose to give to others and yourself are what define you. Accept your narrative as evidence of your tenacity rather than as a burden.

By doing this, you will only liberate yourself but also encourage others to follow suit.

Chapter 14
Game Changer

Have you ever had a moment when you knew everything had to change? I remember sitting on the edge of my bed that one night, staring at my reflection in that dim glow of a desk lamp. My life really felt like a series of closed doors and missed opportunities. The weight of poverty, self-doubt, and circumstances beyond my control I had allowed to shape my story for far too long. But that night was different. I grabbed my worn-down notebook and wrote out my affirmations, speaking each one as if my life depended on it—because it did. Then, I made a decision that changed everything: I invested in myself. I enrolled in college, not just for a degree, but to rewrite my story. That decision wasn't just for me; it was for every person who ever thought they couldn't rise above their circumstances. This isn't about where I was—it's about where I decided to go and how you can make the same decision to change your game.

For years, I felt like life was something that happened to me, not something I had control over. I had convinced myself that success was for other people—those who didn't grow up in poverty, who didn't carry the weight of their past on their shoulders. But one day, it hit me: I was waiting for a change that only I could create. That realization was both terrifying and liberating. The fear of inadequacy whispered, What if you're not smart enough? What if you fail? But I realized I was already failing by not trying.

The first step was small but powerful: I started speaking affirmations over my life every day. I wrote down phrases like I am capable, I am deserving, and I am enough and repeated them until I believed them. Faith became my anchor—I prayed for guidance and trusted that God had bigger plans for me than my circumstances. Then, I made a tangible commitment to growth: I enrolled in school to pursue a degree in social work. It wasn't just about education; it was about proving to myself that I could rise above my doubts and fears.

I also built habits that kept me grounded and focused. Every morning, I started with gratitude, writing down three things for which I was thankful. I listened to motivational speakers like Les Brown and Dr. Eric Thomas, who reminded me that my story could inspire others if I were brave enough to share it. Slowly but surely, these tools became the foundation of my journey. They didn't just help me grow; they taught me how to thrive. That was the turning point—the moment I chose to believe in myself, even when it felt impossible. And that choice has made all the difference.

It was like entering a new world as I began my path to obtaining a social work degree. I merely had the will to go forward; I had no road map. The difficulties quickly arose balancing personal obligations, employment obligations, and schoolwork was extremely taxing. There were evenings when I wanted to give up because I was so tired, but I knew deep down that I couldn't. I discovered how to overcome my doubts by reminding myself that this degree was a gateway to changing the world, not just a piece of paper.

I didn't realize I had the discipline needed to juggle my studies and the responsibilities of life. Setting boundaries and prioritizing my time allowed me to say no to distractions and yes to opportunities that matched my objectives. There were moments when I thought I was failing at everything, including work, school, and being there for the people I loved, but I eventually realized that persistence just meant not giving up, not being flawless.

Despite the difficulties, I also had victories that justified all of my sacrifices. I experienced the effects of my choice to become a social worker for the first time when I applied a lesson I had learned in class to a real-world scenario. Every job finished and paper turned in was a tiny win that boosted my self-esteem.

My greatest teacher turned out to be adversity. It taught me that discomfort is a necessary part of progress, and that tenacity is a daily choice rather than a destination. I discovered that strength is about getting back up when you feel like you're going to fall, not about never struggling. And every time I did, I felt a bit stronger and more confident that I was headed in the right direction.

A distinct vision for my life started to take shape as I worked on my personal growth and strengthened my faith in God. My hardships served as more than simply roadblocks; they served as steppingstones that may lead others to change and hope. I gained a deep feeling of purpose from this insight, and I learned that telling my story was not only therapeutic for me but also a lifeline for others.

My first public speaking experiences were nerve-racking and humiliating. I spoke my truth in front of small groups of people, and I saw how my comments spoke to those who felt stuck in their situation. I learned the value of meeting people where they are and the strength of vulnerability from those experiences. Every time I spoke, my confidence in my capacity to connect—not just through words, but also through our common struggles and victories—grew.

I worked to gain coaching experience from legendary speakers like Les Brown and Dr. Eric Thomas as a result of this journey, and their guidance sparked my development. They forced me to delve farther, polish my message, and present it with authenticity and passion. Les taught me how to make every word matter in a story by using emotion. I learned how to light a fire inside people from ET, inspiring them to take action and believe in themselves.

I learned how to reach from these mentors, not just how to speak. They taught me how to stay true to my main goal while modifying my message for a variety of audiences. I had personal breakthroughs under their direction that gave me more self-assurance and clarity.

During this process, I came to understand that storytelling is about illustrating what is possible rather than only retelling occurrences. And even as I keep learning and developing, my goal is still to show people that they, too, have the power to transform their own lives, overcome their obstacles, and rewrite their own narratives.

Witnessing the transformation of lives through the power of action and hope has been the most fulfilling aspect of my journey. People I've met over the years have found the strength to confront their own challenges after hearing my personal story. There is the young man who went back to school after realizing his potential, and the single mother who launched her own company after years of feeling she would never be able to escape poverty. These stories serve as a reminder to me that when one individual succeeds, it sets off a domino effect that empowers families and communities.

The influence has expanded beyond individual lives to include programs meant to end cycles of desperation and poverty. Through community projects, speaking engagements, and workshops, I've been able to establish spaces where individuals may set objectives, dream anew, and move forward toward a better future. Every success story spreads the word, demonstrating to others that change is not only feasible but also achievable.

However, I'm not the only one who can change the game. This is a call to action for everyone who reads it: have faith in your God-given destiny, believe in yourself, and take the first step toward a better world. Perseverance, faith, and affirmations are more than simply words; they are instruments that can change people's lives.

My goal for the future is very clear: to keep expanding, reach more people, and provide the next generation the tools they need to overcome their current situation. I'm dedicated to assisting people in realizing that their ability to overcome obstacles defines them rather than their challenges. One story, one community, and one life at a time, we can alter the game together. I now give you this task: What will be your initial action? You must take action because the game won't change on its own.

When I think back on this journey, I am really thankful for the challenges that helped me develop, the successes that let me remember why I was here, and the progress that stretched me. All of this would not have been possible without faith, tenacity, and the supportive voices that reverberated throughout my life, particularly those of my grandmother Bertha. She never doubted me, even when I did. Her unshakable faith in me gave me the courage and willpower I still rely on today. She used to say to me, "You were created for something bigger than what you can see now." Keep going. Even though Grams is no longer with me, her words continue to direct me.

This phase of my life is proof of resilience—of overcoming obstacles and escaping the constraints imposed on us by external events or self-doubt. It serves as a reminder that you have the ability to change your story, regardless of where you begin. Affirmations gave me the confidence to dream, perseverance gave me the strength to act, and faith in God provided me the foundation to remain firm.

I want everyone who reads this to know that they possess the same power. Your hardships are the start of something bigger, not the end. Will you be the first to take action? Will you have the courage to have the same faith in yourself that my grandma had in me? Your game-changing moment is waiting—it's time to make the move.

For everybody who has ever felt hopeless, ignored, or stuck, this is a narrative of hope, not just mine. I will leave you with this: What will be the moment that changes your game? The world is ready for you to get up.

Acknowledgements

I want to start by giving thanks to God for His constant love, grace, and direction along this journey. I've been able to face my reality and let go of the grief I once carried by trusting His process. I will always be thankful to Him for giving me purpose, strength, and healing.

Thank you, family, for giving me the time and grace to process my life through these writings. Especially my kids, who gave up valuable time with me while I focused on this task, your understanding and patience have been an invaluable asset.

I am deeply grateful to all those who encouraged, pushed, and inspired me to face my healing journey head-on. Even when I doubted myself, your confidence in me kept me going. You served as my compass when I felt lost, and I am grateful to my accountability partners for ensuring that I remained focused and followed through.

Paula with gratitude I thank you from the bottom of my heart—I'm not even sure where to start. You came into my life with a light that cut through my darkness when I was at my lowest point and the burden of everything felt too heavy. You genuinely saw me, prayed for me, and prayed with me—you didn't simply hear my suffering.

When I felt hopeless, your courage, faith, and willingness to share your personal story gave me hope. Even when I couldn't see it for myself, you helped me realize that there was still a way forward and reminded me that my life matters. I started going to therapy and took it seriously because of you. It has changed my life, and without you, I don't think I would have gotten this far.

Paula, you saved my life. I will always remember your faith, love, and compassion as a lifeline. God put you in my life at the perfect time, and I am so thankful for that. I appreciate your belief in me during a time when I was unable to trust in myself. You will always hold a particular place in my heart, and I hope that others may be blessed by your generosity and light in the same manner that you have blessed me.

I'm grateful to my college English professor for seeing my potential when I didn't, as well as to all of the coaches and mentors who helped me step outside of my comfort zone and taught me how to invest in and believe in myself. Your advice has changed my life.

I'm incredibly grateful to my beloved group of supporters who listened to me read chapter after chapter, however many times I did, and to the brilliant brains who shared innumerable sleepless nights. This book would not have been possible without your suggestions, support, and insight.

Finally, I want to thank my readers for opening this book and immersing themselves in my story. I am so grateful for your support. I hope Nothing Silent Anymore speaks to you and serves as a reminder that your voice, your truth, and your journey toward healing are important.

Made in the USA
Monee, IL
17 February 2025

b5604ac9-89f6-4607-a393-23ae8ff1ced9R01